CHILD OF THE CUSP

by
Gurutej Singh Khalsa

Cover Credits:

Photo of the Blind Walk, a White Tantric Yoga kriya, superimposed over the painting "And the Sun Shall Rise in the West" by Ravi Tej Singh Khalsa. Conception by Gurutej Singh Khalsa. Realization by Gurumustuk Singh Khalsa and Dev Dharam Kaur Khalsa.

Photograph Credits:

"Starry-Eyed and Untried" - Soorya Kaur Khalsa
"A Few Steps on the Path" - Soorya Kaur Khalsa
"The Hand of the Guru" - Gurumustuk Singh Khalsa
"In Guru's Footsteps" - Soorya Kaur Khalsa
"The Master" - Soorya Kaur Khalsa
"Perspectives of a Pilgrim" - Sardarni Premka Kaur
Back Cover Photo of Author - Peraim Kaur Khalsa

Canadian Cataloguing in Publication Data

Khalsa, Gurutej Singh, 1950-
Children of the cusp

ISBN 1-55212-830-X

1. Harbhajan Singh Khalsa, Yogiji--Poetry.   2. Sikhism--Poetry.   I.
Title.
PS3611.H34C44 2001   811'.6   C2001-911001-4

TRAFFORD

This book was published *on-demand* in cooperation with Trafford Publishing.
On-demand publishing is a unique process and service of making a book available for retail sale to the public taking advantage of on-demand manufacturing and Internet marketing.
On-demand publishing includes promotions, retail sales, manufacturing, order fulfilment, accounting and collecting royalties on behalf of the author.

Suite 6E, 2333 Government St., Victoria, B.C. V8T 4P4, CANADA
Phone   250-383-6864   Toll-free   1-888-232-4444 (Canada & US)
Fax   250-383-6804   E-mail   sales@trafford.com
Web site   www.trafford.com   TRAFFORD PUBLISHING IS A DIVISION OF TRAFFORD HOLDINGS LTD.
Trafford Catalogue #01-0230   www.trafford.com/robots/01-0230.html

10   9   8   7   6   5   4

DEDICATION

This book is humbly dedicated to my Beloved Master, Siri Singh Sahib Bhai Sahib Harbhajan Singh Khalsa Yogiji, who brought the word of the Guru and the sacred science of Kundalini Yoga to the West; to those Children of the Cusp who have made his vision a living reality, and to those Children of the Future who will carry his banner on.

TABLE OF CONTENTS

THE HAND OF THE GURU

IN GURU'S FOOTSTEPS

THE MASTER

PERSPECTIVES OF A PILGRIM

MOMENTS OF SIGNIFICANCE

SIBLINGS OF DESTINY

APPENDIX: THE FIVE KRIYAS

Preface

to

"Children of the Cusp"

by
Yogi Bhajan
(Siri Singh Sahib Harbhajan Singh Khalsa Yogiji)

We are in the cusp period. In this 21 years, which started in 1991, we are moving from the Piscean Age into the Age of Aquarius. During this time, the guardian and the guards have changed, so the tendency in human faculties has to change.

We are entering the Age of Aquarius, and Age of Aquarius means knowledge. What you know in the Piscean age is not going to work in the Aquarian Age. It is the assessment age, the age of self-knowledge; it is the age of enlightenment. Anybody who shall not know the self shall be nothing but miserable.

I came to the west in 1969, not to collect students, but to create teachers. And thus, 3HO Foundation was born, an organization dedicated to making people to live Healthy, Happy & Holy, because I knew that America had to become a spiritual leader of the Age of Aquarius. That's why I hung in here.

We started poor, as young people with no money, and no place. We were born of all rich parents, but we became homeless, and were called the "Woodstock Nation." We banded and were branded as Flower Children. Many died to bring an evolution in America. I participated in that evolution which started from a point of revolution in the '60's, and today, thousands of those hippies have become yuppies. We shall enter the Age of Aquarius and take America with us, cleaner, better, stronger and gracious, and God-loving nation, not God fearing. The change will be: from God-fearing to God-loving.

It is now the Cusp of the Age of Aquarius. It is not Piscean age, and all those who belong to the Piscean age shall die, will disappear. And everywhere you will hear things that you do not expect to hear.

Enter the Age of Aquarius with positive affirmation, and nothing can go wrong. Your insecurities are your insecurities, and your shortcomings are shortcomings. But who in the world doesn't have them? You are greater than your problems.

Always remember you have a face and you have a grace. If you can remember these two things, and live up to it, you will never be sorry. Identify yourself with grace, always. Keep your face as good as God is, and everything will come to you.

Every age has its story, and this is the story of many of the men and women who have risen to usher in the Age of Aquarius in a new light. This is our story, the Children of the Cusp.

CHILDREN OF THE CUSP

We are the ones who have no place,
Who've come to challenge time and space,
We've come to go, for we don't belong,
Yet, we shall write Victory's song,
We, the Children of the Cusp.

We live between the ages, out and in,
The Age of Aquarius we shall begin,
The Age of Pisces we shall lay to rest,
We came; we tried and gave our best,
We, the Children of the Cusp.

For the Age of Aquarius we are obsolete,
For those criteria we fail to meet,
For the Age of Pisces we have no place,
Our minds too vast for that slow pace,
We, the Children of the Cusp.

All we are is what we create,
That attempt alone makes us great
And the sacrifices that we make
Have changed to Destiny, from Fate,
We, the Children of the Cusp.

We belong nowhere else but here
And this sacred trust we hold dear,
To lay down the consecrated foundation
Of our Sovereign Khalsa Spiritual Nation!
We, the Children of the Cusp.

Let no one misunderstand who we are,
There is no magic or mystical star,
We're not aliens who've come from space
And it's only here that we have a place,
We, the Children of the Cusp.

We were carved from the mud by God's hand,
And given the breath so we could stand
To do the work of Destiny's call
And for that, we have given all.
We, the Children of the Cusp.

Many there are who tried their hand,
Many have fallen, who failed to stand,
Yet there are none who have come in vain,
None who shall be remembered with shame,
All are Children of the Cusp.

We have come to see this through,
We do it for us, but mostly for you,
It's not we who are great, but what we do
And we only do it because we have to!
We, the Children of the Cusp.

Espanola
2 March, 1994

INTRODUCTION

On November 22nd, 1993, I was asked to write a poem for the 40th anniversary celebration of the marriage of Siri Singh Sahib Bhai Sahib Harbhajan Singh Khalsa Yogiji and his wife, Siri Sardarni Sahiba Bibi Inderjit Kaur; Yogiji and Bibiji. I was not known as a great poet at that time, but was considered a pretty good writer. From time to time I had written various pieces for different occasions within the activities of Sikh Dharma and 3HO such as announcements, a few official letters, and an occasional article. But I was not really a poet.

It is interesting how the hand of Destiny can move to change the course of a person's life; and on that day, the course of my life changed. So, I put my ego into it and knocked out a five-stanza poem in less than an hour. It sounded pretty good to me and as the day wore on, I polished it a little more. In my car, I drove around reciting until it felt right. I later recited the poem, with some drama, in the Gurdwara, and I was surprised to see that many people had tears in their eyes when I finished. That poem, "The Ruby of the Heart," is found in this book.

After the hukam, the Siri Singh Sahib announced I should write a book of poetry that would describe our history -- the history of Sikh Dharma in the West, as well as the evolution of Guru's message to the world. His directive to me was that it should be 108 poems and should be completed in time to be published for Baisakhi 1995. If I failed, he told me, I would be banished. Then he added, "This is my gift to you."

I calculated that I would have to write a poem a day in order to meet that deadline. This seemed like a piece of cake since I had knocked out the poem that day in less than an hour. However, I did not complete another poem for four months.

I would sit and scratch out a line or couplet, sometimes a stanza, but it did not come together in a cohesive way. I began to doubt if I was really up to this project and questioned if I would succeed. My beloved wife, Sadhana Kaur, bought me a nice notebook with pictures of planets and stars on it so I could scratch out my masterpiece. Mostly though, I scratched out vague lines, no poems. Then one February morning, as I sat fuming at the table trying to produce at least one poem, she came to me, took my pen and wrote on the page in her lovely Italian way, *"Gurutejino you are o.k.!"* That action, a simple loving touch, gave me hope and I knew I was close.

The next evening I was outside the Gurdwara in Espanola and had the idea that I should ask Baba Siri Chand for help. Baba Siri Chand was the son of Guru Nanak, and was the greatest yogi who ever lived. I bowed before the bronze statue of Baba Siri Chand, placed my forehead on his left big toe and asked for his help. I reasoned with Babaji that he had helped Guru Arjan complete the Sukhmani Sahib, the beautiful Psalm of Peace, and all I was asking for was a few poems; to assist me with that should be effortless for so great a soul as he. The cold of that bronze statue seemed to penetrate my brain as I pressed my forehead against Babaji's big toe. The next day no poem came.

The day after, though, I felt something stir deep inside, and the poem, "CHILDREN OF THE CUSP," flowed out. I knew this was to be the title poem of the book and that the flow had begun. That night I read the poem after Yogiji's class and people responded very favorably to it. Thereafter, the poems flowed steadily. Whenever I was blocked, I would ask Baba Siri Chand for help and the next line would come. I am deeply grateful for his kind and compassionate help, which allowed the succeeding poems to flow without the interference of my ego.

Still, it took three years to complete the 108 poems. At one point the Siri Singh Sahib even wrote me a letter, saying that I was working too slowly, (a complaint I have often heard from him). He was encouraging me to hurry up. I tried, but these poems came at their own pace. However, it became a tradition that I would read a new poem after every one of his meditation classes. Having a poem for class was a great motivator for me, and many of the poems in this book were written just an hour or two before class. I was often late, trying to finish in time.

In rereading them while editing, I can clearly see the haste with which many of them were written. Some of the rhymes may seem forced and are even repeated in more than one poem. However, mostly I have left them as they were written and recited in class. After all, there are not many words that rhyme with life. More than one poem refers to "the call". That has many implications such as call of duty, call of destiny, and call of the higher self to act righteously, which fit the theme of several poems. The Siri Singh Sahib was right; this project was a gift he gave to me. The flow of the poetry and the depth of the material are truly by the hand of Grace.

I wanted the poems to be about real things, real experiences and the practical reality of spiritual life at this time, this transition of Ages at the end of the Millennium. I have, of course, taken many poetic liberties and have enjoyed each opportunity to do so. Most of the poems are written from the perspective of a struggling student on the spiritual path at a very weird time in history. The Siri Singh Sahib once told me, "You have been through the hell of it. Now write about it." While many of the poems are subjective, based on my personal experiences and musings, I have found that people relate to them. I believe it is because the challenges and confrontations I have faced are shared by others on this path, in one form or another, and are the common experiences that bind us together.

The writing of these 108 poems has been a process of personal transformation for me, both in my maturity as a poet and teacher, and in my depth of understanding of the teachings. Each poem has its own personality and each evolved in its own way. Each poem told me when it was finished, or when it needed to say more. And with the creation of each, I learned something more, understood something more and developed myself a little more. This was the gift the Siri Singh Sahib gave me. It was not the book or the poems, for they are the *result* of the process. It was the process, itself, and the evolution that occurred in my own psyche that was the true gift. The poetry is my gift in return, and is small compared to what I received.

They came at various times. Once, I wanted to write a poem before class and tried to force something out. I punched away at my keyboard for an hour or more, then gave up, deciding there would be no poem that night. As I was putting on my jacket to walk to class, a line came into my head; then the rest of the poem flowed. I sat and first wrote it out by hand, then fired up my computer, banged it out, and rushed to class. There were many times when I pulled over on the shoulder of the highway between Albuquerque and Santa Fe to write down the lines that begin several of these poems. A few were begun on airplanes, as well. It was not an act of love that wrote them; it was an act of love that sent them to me.

Many of the poems describe the relationship between a Master and a student, something that is not understood here in the West. This is a most sacred and essential relationship, for it falls upon the Master to pull out of the student those elements of his personality that interfere with his own excellence. So, the Master wades into the cesspool of the student's psyche and scrapes clean the walls of his consciousness. It is not the kind of benign (*Well done, Grasshopper*) relationship that we in the West have seen on TV. It is the ultimate sacrifice on the part of the teacher and a most intimate relationship between the Master and the student. Yogiji has said many times that the relationship between Master and student is that of a chisel to a stone. I have not given my Master an easy time of it, as much of this poetry reflects, and I will be eternally grateful to him for his selflessness and unwillingness to give up on me, though I have given up on myself many times. Without my Master, this book would not exist. In fact, the development of this book is a testament to his patience, for I am more than three years behind schedule and he has not yet banished me.

There are many references to Guru. Guru is that power of wisdom and knowledge that gives the disciple enlightenment; that living experience of God. God is like a giant mainframe computer that uses a very sophisticated language, because His calculations are so complex, fast and accurate. Guru is like a smaller mainframe computer that speaks the God language and can translate that language to a more readily comprehensible language. The Master is like a larger computer network that can translate those languages to the Basic PC language the student understands. Yet, when the Master establishes the link between the student and the Guru, there is direct communication with God. Guru is not a personality, for it is not a man. Rather, it is an energy, which is found in the shabd, or sound. It is by reciting those sounds, which are the language of the God computer, that we gain the capacity to make that link.

There is also reference to the Gurus of Sikh Dharma. These were the men who facilitated the establishment of the Guru on the Earth; who embodied that energy for a brief time. In the Age of Aquarius, Guru is not in the form of a man but in its primal form, which is the sound or shabd. There are several poems that describe this or try to explain it in some way. I have always felt that an object of poetry is to challenge the reader. If you will read these poems, that understanding will come.

There are many who deserve to be thanked for their input and encouragement while these poems were being written, though they cannot all be named. The Siri Singh Sahib Bhai Sahib Harbhajan Singh Khalsa Yogiji heads the list. He has guided me, driven me and inspired me to write these lines for the children of the future. The only way a student can truly express his gratitude to his teacher is to become 10 times greater than the teacher and be a great teacher himself. It is my humble prayer that through this book, many will be inspired along the path of consciousness.

My beloved Sadhana Kaur was also a great support and constructive critic when the lines were dumb or the rhymes were contrived. Shanti Kaur Khalsa, my longtime friend, associate and fellow writer, was immensely helpful with her input, although I doubt that she realizes the extent of her contribution. A special thanks goes to Tej Kaur Khalsa who pushed me at the end to take this collection of loose poems and form it into something that made sense and who helped to give shape to the book. Most especially, though, I want to humbly, from the depth of my heart, thank the sangats of Espanola and Los Angeles. It was to them that most of these poems were read and I cannot give enough thanks to all who came to me and expressed their appreciation and personal experiences when they heard the poetry. This is, without question, a collective effort. All I did was hold the pen or punch the keys, the sangat itself wrote the poems.

Finally, I would add this: *Children of the Cusp* is a book of poetry and poetry is meant to be recited. Please do not content yourself with reading, silently, these poems. Recite them aloud, to yourself, to your dog, to your loved ones and friends. The poems will take on a deeper meaning if you do. There are challenges with rhythm and rhyme which, when you recite, become enjoyable and drive the poetry forward.

Few people in this Age and at this point of transition of Ages have been blessed as I have. My gratitude is to all, to the great Akal Purkh, to my beloved teacher and to you, the Children of the Cusp, and the Children of the Future.

Gurutej Singh Khalsa
Los Angeles, California
26 May, 1997

A LITTLE MORE

It is now June of 2001; over four years since the writing of
this book was completed. It has never been published before
now and I must confess that I haven't tried that hard to get it
done, for various reasons. Now, however, the circumstances of
Time and Space seem right and by Guru's Grace, it is finally
done. All of the above still applies, perhaps even more so than
in 1997.

One reference has changed, since 1997. What was referred to
Takht a Khalsa, the gurdwara in Espanola, is now known as
Singhasan a Khalsa.

In some of the poems there are references to other
religions. Nothing in this work is intended to demean or insult
other religions. My points are simply that religion, when it is
formalized, tends to drift away from the essence of the original
teachings. This happens in organized religion, including Sikh
Dharma, as the poem *Sardar ji* implies. What is important is
that any religion, any spiritual path, be practiced with
devotion. It is the individual practice, the power of the
individual prayer and meditation, which give the experience to
the practitioner. When we practice in the company of others
we become a congregation and the individual experience can
be amplified. Sometimes, though, groups can become zealous,
territorial, and intolerant, especially when they perceive that
other religions might be encroaching on what they consider to

be their space; perhaps more appropriately, their source of income.

While there is no intent to insult or discount other religions or spiritual paths, there *is* the intent to emphasize Sikh Dharma. Ultimately, though, these poems are about my personal experiences on a spiritual path and I believe that anyone who walks any spiritual path may be able to relate to those experiences and insights. I think the experience of consciousness is not that different for any one. It is how we frame it in our own psyche and how we carry the awareness and spiritual experience into the ongoing process of living in a big and frequently confusing world that is the real measure of consciousness. The challenge is not to see God, but to see God in All.

There are some poems that refer to the sword in various ways, such as "the grace of the sword". The sword is a powerful symbol in Sikh Dharma. It represents the power of Truth for it cuts both ways. It also symbolizes inner strength, the raising of consciousness as the raising of the Kundalini, and the sharp edge of discrimination upon which those who follow a spiritual path must tread. It also refers to the use of spiritual power. The sword represents the Sarb Shakti or manifest power of the Cosmos. Misuse of that power, like the misuse of a weapon, can have unfortunate consequences. References to the sword are not intended to imply forcible conversion.

One last note: In the poem *The Victory*, the last line of the fifth stanza reads *"Or will the glow with Guru's spark."* I originally wrote it as *"Or will they burn with Guru's spark."* When I read the poem in class, Yogi ji suggested that I change *burn* to *glow*. Obviously a better choice of words for the idea intended.

Please read and *recite* and enjoy. And please share with me your feelings and experiences with the poetry at *gurutej@kiit.com*.

Gurutej Singh Khalsa
Espanola, New Mexico
5 June, 2001

THE STORY

THE STORY

The Immortal God sat in His Grace,
Relaxed in the Infinite, His dwelling place.
He sang to Himself His songs of cheer,
Though He realized there was no one to hear
How sweetly He sang, or to hear His laugh ring
Though He knew He was alone, He continued to sing.
No song was repeated, no words were the same,
But each song He sang was a song of His Name.   -I-

From those sacred sounds that fell from His mouth
He formed the Creation, the North and the South,
Those infinite vibrations formed the East and the West,
He formed the Sun, Moon and Stars, by far His best.
He created the Heavens where the angels would dwell,
Then just for a laugh He created the demons and Hell!
The deities He created to serve Him His tea,
Then He formed up the mountains and brewed up the sea.   -II-

The planets He formed and spun them around stars,
He created the Earth, Jupiter, Saturn and Mars,
He spilled the galaxies across the carpet of the night,
Then when He was ready, He created the Light.
Still, He kept the darkness, for each thing has its place
And in His finest masterstroke, He created Time and Space
And continued to sing with the joy of His heart,
For what He created was the ultimate work of art.   -III-

The deities He loved as they wandered around,
Then they stumbled into Hell, where the demons they found!
He laughed when that happened (He was getting bored),
And when they started to fight He laughed 'til he roared.
Still, there was more that He could form and create,
So drawing in His breath He began to meditate.
Deities and demons caused Him to laugh with mirth,
But still He was not complete, so He looked to planet Earth.   -IV-

An idea struck Him; He knew what to do,
As He regarded the Earth green, white and blue,
He studied His creation, the sky and the sea,
Then thought to Himself, "I can't make another Me!?
"Yet, I'm Omnipotent, unlimited and vast,
For all this Universe I created so fast,
There must be much more to Me than I know,
I'll create another form, then to the Earth I'll go."   -V-

The deities and demons and all of their chelas
Made a yatra to Earth in the first kumba mela.
He divided Himself into three, but remained One,
"I *must* be Great because look what I've done!
One to Generate and get this creation to go,
One to Organize, to sustain and make it to grow,
One to Destroy or Deliver, we'll see,
What a wonderful creation this is, by Me!"   -VI-

The deities set up shop and began running around,
And the demons set to work tearing it down,
They fought and they feuded, such a passion play!
But their quest for power was getting in the way,
"Time to complete it, time to make Myself whole,
Time to push further, yet maintain Self control,
Time for a way to return to My primal sound,
So only on Earth will that chance be found."   -VII-

So taking the mud, He heated it with fire,
Then threw it through the air, higher and higher,
It spun and it grew, creating a great sound,
Then landed on Earth and the creatures were found!
In His deepest expression of Love, He gave each of them
His sweet sacred kiss, then the breath they drew in,
They flew through the sky; they crawled over the land,
They swam in the sea, then some started to stand.   -VIII-

He smiled when He saw them, He laughed with great joy,
"I feel so happy, like an innocent young boy!"
He stopped in his tracks, "Now that's the next thing,
I'll create Mankind and my Name we'll all sing!"
From within His own heart he squeezed His Divine blood,
"I would walk on this Earth Myself, if I could,
But those who are Human will walk in My place
And by calling My Name, they'll all see My Face!"   -IX-

"Yes!" He thought, "Then they'll know they are Me!
I mean, I am only One, but I'll be fun to see!"
Then He turned to the deities, "Look here, My dears,
These humans you must guide to Me, through their fears,
Bring them together with care, then bring them to Me
And don't fight with the demons; they'll get in the way, you see.
This is all I ask of you, for I do love you too,
So do this with Love, you must see it through."   -X-

So to the human creatures the deities reached,
And they began to guide them, they began to teach
The use of the breath and the power of the Word;
Those sacred sounds which bring bliss when heard.
And Mankind grew in consciousness and grace,
It was there in the heavens and on Earth in each face
And deep in each human the Infinite power was given,
For there, behind the navel, the Kundalini was hidden.   -XI-

Then, in each human the Serpent rose to join her Lord
And all of Mankind bowed in reverence to the Word,
For the sacred Kundalini, the coil of the lover,
Unwinds and rises, spreading her hood over
The arc of the Man who to her remains true,
Giving wisdom and knowledge - some called them Guru,
But this is the right and privilege of each soul:
To raise the Kundalini; to be complete and whole.   -XII-

4

Throughout the Universe all the beings sang His praise,
For the joy of the Ages and their spirits to raise,
The angels hovered low as Mankind began to rise,
And prayed to Akal Purkh to give them the prize
Of the human incarnation and the gift of the soul;
That they could join with Him and together be whole,
For it is only on the Earth that exists the Law of Karma,
And the only way to avoid it is upon the path of Dharma.   -XIII-

Of all His Creation there was none more dear
Than the tiny little man whose prayer He would hear,
The prayer of the innocent, the prayer of the heart,
The prayer of longing caused His blessings to start.
Then the deities and demons began to see
How innocent and gullible Mankind could be,
So out of their jealousy they began to deceive,
And eventually Mankind they began to mislead.   -XIV-

Rather than show the way to the Infinite Creator,
The deities gave powers; God could come later.
So in the quest for power Mankind lost his way,
While the deities rose before him to lead him astray,
They told the innocent man that *they* were the Whole
And in the worship of the deities, Mankind lost his Soul
And forgot that he is Infinite and to whom he belonged,
But the great Akal Purkh kept singing *His* song.   -XV-

"Time for a change then, it's Time to recreate,
After all, I am God and my Creation is great!
I'll transform myself and touch this world of form,
I'll take a physical body and as a human I'll be born,
I'll set a clear path; in fact I'll make two
So whatever the personality, Man can find his way through."
He pulled Himself up; He focused in His heart,
Then loosed that Infinite Energy and let the next Age start.   -XVI-

5

From the Infinite Creator two Divine channels grew,
"One I'll call Jewish and the other one Hindu."
To each He gave His secrets; to each He gave a Way
For Mankind to track his life, so God could watch His play,
To each He put His tests to challenge every Soul,
To touch that place of reverence that makes the Spirit whole.
"Have no fear, my children, you'll always have a guide,
I'll walk on Earth among you, I'm always by your side."   -XVII-

In the desert the Jews walked in circles for forty years;
To release them from their bondage and free them from their fears.
He gave the Ten Commandments to test them to the hilt,
But because they could not keep them, the Jews created guilt.
Some became ascetics and lived in caves by trickling streams,
They guarded the ancient secrets and were known as the Essenes,
Who understood the Universe and technology of the mind,
But they kept those secrets hidden, bringing pain upon
Mankind.   .-XVIII-

The Hindus understood the order of life for Man,
Those intricate principals by which the Universe ran;
That Divine technology and how it should be applied,
But they kept that knowledge secret, rather than to guide
The people through their lives, to free them from their pain,
They kept the masses downtrodden so only a few would gain.
They kept the worship of the deities to pacify the masses,
Then divided the society into limited castes and classes.   -XIX-

God took many incarnations to make His message clear,
He walked upon the Earth with those He held so dear.
Through all of His channels he had many forms and faces,
He appeared to many people in many lands and places,
He always showed the way and He was known by many Names
And in each earthly situation His message remained unchanged,
"The Truth lies there within you, though you look for it outside,
Meditate upon my Word and forget your foolish pride."   -XX-

Gautam was a Hindu, a privileged and pampered youth,
Who saw how Mankind suffered and sought to know the Truth
Of why it is we suffer and what is the way to be free,
So he left his pampered life and sat down under a tree;
To meditate for an answer, to try to ease the pain,
And after many long years, Enlightenment was what he gained.
He became known as the Buddha and walked the Middle Way,
Until by his own disciple, he was poisoned and betrayed.   -XXI-

Through the land of Israel walked a Nazarene,
Who openly taught the people the secrets of the Essenes.
He taught the common people, opening up their eyes
To the desecration of the Temples and corruption of the rabbis,
He screamed loudly to the masses, "Heal Yourselves, don't look
back!"
Then he was betrayed and stretched like a hide upon a rack
And from within his breaking heart he cried into the blue,
"Forgive them all, my Father, for they don't know what
they do!"   -XXII-

That simple act of compassion from that humble man,
Started a chain reaction that spread throughout all lands,
But what is before the people is not what Jesus taught,
For another form of control is what the clergy sought
And by the sixth century the essence of Christianity was lost,
Then upon a sea of guilt her congregations were tossed.
So as the course of History stumbled forward with a lurch,
The falling Roman Empire became the Holy Catholic Church. -XXIII-

Out there in the desert that had been circled by the Jews,
A man called Hazrat Mohammed began to spread the news
Among the tribes of the desert that had been left behind,
That the One God stands with us and He is Merciful and Kind,
Allah is how He is called, its plain for the faithful to see,
Spread the news across the world and kill all who disagree.
So, like flames before the wind, Islam spread across the world,
Then into wars of religion Mankind was stupidly hurled.   -XXIV-

The Hindus attacked the Buddhists and killed them where they stood,
The Muslims killed the Hindus and bathed the idols with their blood,
The Christians fought the Muslims, sending their own children into war,
Then turned on their congregations, spreading the Inquisition far.
The monks hid in the monasteries, the Yogis hid in their caves,
While the priests, pundits and mullahs sent thousands to their graves
And huge cults of personality were built around those men:
The ones called Avatars, whom God had entered in.   -XXV-

"Well," he thought to Himself, "it's Time to make a change,
Time for some adjustments, Time to rearrange,
Time to start the transition into another Age,
Time for the course of History to turn another page."
Then He looked into himself, "So let the process start!"
And He meditated profoundly, probing deep into His Heart,
"All those who I've sent to carry the message in My Name,
Left cults of personality and the Truth is lost, to their shame." -XXVI-

"All I ever wanted was for them to worship the Sound;
That is their True Identity and the Way that I am found.
They cannot worship a man, or an idol or a stone,
They must direct themselves by that experience which is known,
The time for Faith is passing; the Time for Truth has come,
Time to give the straight course, to find the fastest way home.
I will roll myself into the Shabd Guru
So all who bow can find their way through."   -XXVII-

The Father of the Bedis was given the call to begin
To ignite the Light of Wisdom within the hearts of Men,
He took the incarnation and laughed out loud at his birth,
For he brought the Shabd Guru to life on planet Earth,
He stepped into the river and dived deep into his soul
And emerged as Guru Nanak with the Universe in his control,
"There is no Hindu or Mussalman for the Immortal God is One."
Then he began to weave all the channels into a single one.   -XXVIII-

Guru Nanak found one disciple; through every test he stood true,
So the one known as Bhai Lena, became Angad, the Guru.
Guru Angad spread the message that Guru Nanak had given,
And formed the Gurmukhi script so the Shabds could be written,
He missed Guru Nanak so painfully that he locked himself away
In a tiny little room, where he could meditate day to day,
Yet without the True Guru, a Sikh has no hope or life,
Then his Sikhs found the Guru and their love removed his strife.

-XXIX-

There was an old man who for twelve years served the True Guru,
Then set out in the darkness on a night when a cold wind blew,
On his back he carried Guru's water through that dark and cold,
Then Guru Angad blessed him saying, "The Guruship now *you* hold!"
Oh, Honor of the Honorless, we call on Guru Amar Das,
Oh, Hope of the Hopeless, we call on Guru Amar Das,
Oh, Shelter of the Shelterless, we call on Guru Amar Das,
Strength to the Weak and Lost is Guru Amar Das.   -XXX-

Jetha was an orphan, the streets of Goindwal he walked alone,
Then Guru Amar Das blessed him and gave him shelter in his home,
He served the Guru's langar with divine humility and grace,
Then Guru tested his heart and gave him the Guru's place.
Guru Ram Das, Sodhi Sultan, gave to the world the Sarover,
Where those with a prayer, though beaten at heart,
find the hope to start over,
Guru of Miracles is Guru Ram Das and his temple is open to all,
Then he passed the flame after seven years and Arjan
answered the call.   -XXXI-

Guru Arjan took the Word and gave it a definite form
For by his hand, in perfect *Raag,* the Adi Granth was born,
Then to turn the Destiny to meet the coming Age,
He sat upon the hot plate, a serene and humble sage.
He sacrificed himself to show us the way that's right,
Then passed on to his son the Shabd Guru's Light,
So as Guru Arjan Dev quietly met his end,
Young Bhandi Chor became Guru Hargobind.   -XXXII-

The master of the world, the master of the soul,
This is the way of a Sikh to be complete and whole.
He established the Holy Akal Takht, wearing two ringing swords,
To be the temporal world's master and her spiritual lord,
Bidi Chand brought Dilbagh and Gulbagh to Guru's door,
And when the Sultan heard it, his army went to war,
But the army of Guru Hargobind stood and faced the fight
And sent the Moguls running into that cold, dark night.   -XXXIII-

Holy Guru Har Rai was gentle and kind,
With a compassionate heart and a humble mind,
He kept a standing army, though the animals he loved,
For the Law of Compassion is how the spirit is proved.
Then Guru Har Krishan, a beautiful child of five,
Kept the Radiant Light of Guru Nanak alive.
There at Bangla Sahib, he took on himself the plague,
And the painful suffering of thousands, by that
sacrifice was saved.   -XXXIV-

For twenty-seven years Guru Hargobind's son
Sat in a tiny room and meditated alone,
In his secret solitude he received the Light of the Guru,
(Although it was a few weeks before anyone knew),
Guru Tegh Bahadur, in his simple grace and peace
Quietly sacrificed himself to bring religious relief,
He bowed, then gave his head and merged into the One,
Then passed the Light of Nanak to Gobind Rai, his son.   -XXXV-

Rishi Dusht Daman, as he was known before,
Was given the *hukam* by God to go to Earth once more:
To finish the job and rearrange the flow,
"But only if You work *through* me will I go."
He created the Khalsa to reign supreme
And through them he became Guru Gobind Singh,
He took the Adi Granth, and made it the Siri Guru,
To guide his beloved Khalsa ever straight and true.   -XXXVI-

Once again, by the Grace of the Sword
Mankind shall bow only to the Word,
Then the Immortal God looked to the West,
"Time to bring out of Myself the best,
Time to unite all the paths I've laid,
Time to redeem all the souls I've made,
Like oil upon water, Guru's word will spread,
So in every land my Precious Ones will be lead."   -XXXVII-

The Time is right now; the New Age has arrived,
Where the way of the Guru is the way to survive.
For God in His perfection took a simple stone
And polished it through the Ages, it is the only One,
Then the sacred Kundalini He carefully placed inside
And set it on the Earth with all His Joy and Pride.
And that gem of a Yogi has brought the Word of the Guru
To all those fallen angels, who are simply, me and you.   -XXXVIII-

Espanola, New Mexico
6 November 1995

11

STARRY-EYED
AND UNTRIED

THE WAY WE WERE

They called us "Freaks" when we first began;
Another strange cult from a foreign land,
Another generation gone astray,
More panhandlers to get in the way.

After Woodstock things began to fall,
What we thought, wasn't Truth at all
And the Great Society's suction machine
Tried to destroy us and kill the dream.

They sent us to war to "Keep the Peace,"
They shot and beat us in the streets,
They watched us die and felt no pain,
But now it is they who live in shame.

There was a cry and there were songs,
A pervasive sense of something wrong,
The immoral war, the cries for Peace;
Total desperation seeking release.

Sex, drugs, and rock 'n roll
Cell by cell they took their toll,
Dazed and confused in Purple Haze,
Smoke and needles; our minds were crazed.

Thousands of Children on the run,
Beardless boys under the gun,
Corruption and betrayal at the top,
Escalating madness that wouldn't stop.

Our cries of anguish, loud and shrill,
Were heard by a Yogi with an Iron Will,
Who walked at Peace within that rage,
A most humble, patient, yet modern sage.

To the City of the Angels he came,
And Yogi Bhajan was his name.
There were many angels in that town
With broken wings, on the ground.

"Heal yourselves, arise and stand
On your own two feet, retake this land!
Have you forgotten who you are?
Don't you see your Rising Star?"

He took those angels with the broken wings
And taught them to fly, to breathe and sing.
And when they began to fly around
He made them move to another town.

We were scattered, broken, across this land
Hiding, with our heads in the sand,
But the patched up angels with fixed up wings
Taught others to fly, to breathe, and sing.

In those early days before we grew,
We were funky, our numbers few,
We were young and full of hope,
Slowly repairing the damage from dope.

But many angels could no longer stand,
And fell, again, into the shifting sand.
Yet many more could make the claim,
"I am broken, yet still I remain!"

We're all that's left of the Woodstock Nation.
We're the Spirit and the Foundation
Of the Cusp of the Aquarian Age,
Repaired by that patient, Iron Willed Sage.

Espanola, New Mexico
28 March, 1994

HOW I BEGAN

This is the story of when I started
To walk this path of the open-hearted,
At a rock festival is where I began
To learn the science of Kundalini
And change myself from a spaced out weenie,
When all I wanted was to hear the bands.

So I started out with a bunch of fools
To rock and roll and break the rules,
But by the "Yoga Tent" was where we camped!
That first morning was a yoga class
Which I walked into, but meant to pass,
And that experience on my mind, was stamped.

They said "The Yogi" would speak that night,
Our hearts and minds he would delight,
And I should be there to know the Truth.
I planned to go for that whole day
But then a few drugs got in the way
And when the time came, well, my mind was loose.

To the "Yoga Tent" I made my way,
To hear what "The Yogi" had to say,
But first there was a yoga class!
Now, yoga and drugs don't really mix
And by the end, I was in a fix,
My heart and mind were running fast.

All my clothes were soaked with sweat
And I was thinking that Tibet
Was the only place where I could be talked down.
Then "The Yogi" began to speak
And I truly began to Freak,
I'll never forget that awesome sound.

He said "You've come to lose your fears",
(I heard with my mind, not my ears),
"And drugs will destroy your Heart and Soul."
Then my Ego screamed into my brain,
"Run you fool, don't bear this pain!"
So I turned and tried to find a hole.

I crawled away on hands and knees
To the edge where I could see
Thousands of aimless people on the strand,
And I knew that in that raging sea
Was not where I was meant to be,
The time had come for me to take a stand.

Then I understood I had found the Door
To what I had prayed my whole life for,
I had to go back and take it like a Man.
Then softly, I began to cry
As my Ego began to die,
While my tears rolled onto the sand.

I turned again and followed the sound
Back to my little piece of ground;
On my hands and knees I returned.
He said, "Now it's the time to grow,
"Forget these drugs and let them go,
This opportunity, you have earned!"

And in myself, I felt a deep Peace,
For my Fears had been released,
I had faced myself and seen my Soul!
So, that is how it began for me
To walk this path to Victory,
But that was many long years ago.

Espanola, New Mexico
14 April 1994

IN 1971

Winter Solstice, Nineteen Seventy-One,
We went to Florida to enjoy the sun
At the ashram of Baba Siri Chand,
Under the green trees, beside the pond.
We set the camp and pitched our tents
To enjoy, together, that great event.

It was a beautiful day in the Sunshine State
To construct the camp and meditate,
Yogiji spoke to us that first morning,
"Be careful what you eat," was his warning.
So we went to the beach, we enjoyed the day,
Then the Sheriff told us that we couldn't stay.

So after dinner we struck the camp,
The evening air was chilly and damp,
We packed the tents as the light grew dark
And prepared to move to a trailer park.
All cars were packed and ready to go
Then one by one, we moved out, slow.

Each car was packed with its full load,
As we moved the convoy onto the road,
One hundred vehicles moved in the night
Past Yogiji, directing with his flashlight,
Standing at the entrance to the Ashram's drive,
He directed the traffic to keep us alive.

We moved across town past the county line,
A long string of cars moving serpentine
Through the streets of the city, our headlights carved their
arc,
Then we stopped at that funky old trailer park.
And the first thing that he told us, before the tents went up,
"Enjoy the Winter Solstice, but avoid that grocery shop!"

The winter night was lovely as we pitched the tents,
Yet many of us were struggling with his last comments,
For the grocery store was open late into the night,
And that temptation was more than most of us could fight,
Plus, chocolate keeps you warm when it's dark and cold,
So, from that little store, every Hershey bar was sold.

That first Winter Solstice was a turning point for me,
So with new inspiration I returned to Tennessee,
For at that funky place in a tent that leaked the rain,
A little spark of Self began to glow inside my brain
And many long years later I can joyfully exclaim,
That little spark inside me has fanned into a Flame!

Espanola, New Mexico
17 January, 1995

FREAKS
OF THE
NEW FRONTIER

Kundalini Yoga, pearls before swine,
This sacred science missed by the blind;
Those who came and were sincere were few,
But many wanted to buy a guru,
To have status in Society's eyes.

For many it was just another trip,
Something groovy, cool and hip,
Plaster casters and the Hollywood folks
Came to the Yogi to get their strokes,
And for them he had a surprise!

A simple little herb that grows in the ground
Can let you know where your friends are found.
Garlic can separate the phony from the true,
So the beautiful people sought another guru,
Then all that was left were the freaks.

Dirty and funky we staggered in,
Doing breath of fire, smelling like sin.
Slowly we began to grow and to change,
But our basic habits he had to rearrange.
He laughs when of that time he speaks.

We learned how to wash, to brush and to comb,
And that God prefers a clean and cozy home,
That underwear has a value, you know
And that crow pose is the right way to go.
Still, we kept the spirit alive.

Banana Ananda and *Golly ji*
Personified our urge to be free.
Long flowing hair and sprouting beards,
While gradually turbans appeared,
Somehow we managed to survive.

We were people without a clue
Of how to live or what to do;
Of how to negotiate our way
Through this life from day to day,
He truly transformed our lives.

Now we have grown, those days are past,
We have built this Dharma, which will last
For thousands upon thousands of years,
Laid down by the Freaks of the New Frontier.
And We have status in Society's eyes!

Espanola, New Mexico
18 May, 1994

THE ASHRAM

Nights in the restaurant 'til midnight,
Scratching the Earth to develop this land,
We built the Dome with our own hands,
Trying our best to get it right.
We've walked this path all these years
Facing ourselves, our doubts and fears.

We got up at four to meditate:
Sadhana couldn't start until
All were present, quiet and still;
Onions and chapatis were all we ate.
Many there were who took a stand,
Who left their mark upon this land.

Sundays we had to work the grounds
After Gurdwara and Langar cleaning
And attendance at the family meeting.
Then, the new week began it's rounds.
Slowly Guru's grinding wheel
Has polished us into shining steel.

We slept in the barn with the mice,
We slept in tents that leaked in the rain,
We survived each summer's transforming refrain
And one year we had a problem with lice.
Slow and steady we have carried on
Laying the foundation and singing our songs.

We married and began family lives.
We had babies who started to grow,
We had chapatis, but we had no dough,
And we usually fought with our wives.
We've carried the banner through thick and thin.
Though it looked like defeat, we knew we would win.

We started businesses to expand our domain.
Though work is a worship we found that success
Doesn't come easy and is a great cause of stress,
In fact it can make you insane!
But Guru's Mission is to be fulfilled
Through Fire of the Test and Strength of the Will.

We suffered the loss of those who we loved,
Those who left with Guru's light upon their face
And those who left through betrayal and disgrace,
Are still remembered, regarded and loved.
Love, which is God, has no Time and Space,
It has no condition or meaningless place.

For all these years through pain, trial and test
We've stood together to lay this Foundation,
For here is the Home of our Khalsa Nation
And for that we shall surely be blessed!
Let all who have longing know this to be True:
Your fulfillment lies here, in the Home of the Guru!

Espanola, New Mexico
9 May, 1994

THE DOOR

We were unaware, way back then
When the Consciousness began to turn,
We were drifting like spores in the wind,
With far to go and much to learn.

The Spirit of Change was in the air
And we breathed deep to get it all.
The Electric excitement and flowing hair,
Then, through the music, we heard the Call.

It took a lot for us to change,
For Discipline was not our Song.
Yet we aimed high to find the Range
And many who started, now are gone.

It seemed so easy at that time
With Peace, Love and Rock and Roll,
But it took more to make that climb;
To open the Heart and free the Soul.

Many looked good and Talked the Talk,
Many carried Trust and Respect,
But only a few could Walk the Walk
And only a few are with us yet.

Now they are calling out in Pain,
They want to return but don't know how.
Can they face Themselves and their Shame,
And before their Guru, humbly bow?

The test of Consciousness, old as Time,
Comes for all who walk this Path.
We each must face it to be Divine;
To know our height, and depth and breadth.

But the Door is not found high above,
For humility is valued above all.
The price we pay is our Love,
So the entrance lies there, low and small.

Many have tried to go around,
Many have thought that they could cheat,
But all must bow, with forehead down,
To have the sight of those Sacred Feet.

Guru's Gate is there for us all,
No one is exempted or rejected.
Those who stand, stumble and fall,
Can recover, return and be respected.

Let them know that only Gratitude
Will sustain them at that time of Test.
To bow with a humble Attitude
Is the only way to achieve our Best.

And let them know that in this House,
The laser beam off the mirror returns,
And those who would treachery espouse
Shall find themselves on a lost sojourn.

We are not false and we are not real,
But no longer do we drift in the wind,
And those who bow, their Souls shall heal,
They shall find the Door and enter in.

Between LA and Espanola, 35,000 feet
1 June, 1994

25 YEARS PAST WOODSTOCK

In the early days before we grew,
Kundalini Yoga was all we knew,
Sikh Dharma was another trip,
Turbans were cool, but hair was hip.

We practiced yoga to get high,
We grew our beards, expecting to fly.
In our breasts beat great hippie hearts,
For the path is easiest wherever it starts.

Solstice in Mendocino, 1972,
He said, "I hand the reigns of the Future to You."
From that point on things began to change,
But our hearts and heads he had to rearrange.

We competed as teachers; our egos were bold,
An effective class was when you passed out, cold.
We began to tie turbans, starch made them right,
And in short little kurtas, we began to wear white.

Along each coast, the East and the West,
The big time ashrams were considered the best.
But through the heartland, in each major town,
The foundation of our Dharma was laid down.

For in the small ashrams of only a few,
The seed of the Guru took root and grew.
Many found courage, with turban and beard,
To face the communities that thought they were weird.

And each morning's sadhana, through cold and dark
Ignited our hippie minds with Guru's spark.
And many years later that light still shines
In our hippie hearts and hippie minds.

Espanola, New Mexico
10 August, 1994

LIVING THROUGH THE CUSP

God, it was so hard way back then,
When my beard was short and I was thin.
It was hard to keep up, hard to smile,
Hard to keep walking for another mile;
Hard to ask for help, we had to be strong,
Hard to find a job or a place to belong
Where it wasn't out of place to be real.

Summer Solstice was always the gauge,
When the course of life turned the page,
Where we puffed up or egos, talking big,
When we sneaked out each night and ate like pigs.
We bragged about our ashrams and how big were our classes,
About how many students were kissing our asses,
Seems it was still out of place to be real.

Like strangers through Time in a land unknown,
We changed ourselves, setting out on our own,
Leaving the past and the culture we knew,
Like the seeds of a willow, on the wind we blew.
Many were lost, but still there were a few
Who began to sprout, then took root and grew;
A weak crop planted in a swamp.

Sideburns became beards and bellbottoms grew tight,
Tie-dyed became solid and solid became white.
Ponytails moved up to the top of the crown
Where, in a coil, our long tresses were wound,
Giving us stature, giving us grace and height
As we began to tie turbans with dismay and delight,
Some with a certain flair and pomp.

The turban became and still today remains
The one thing that can make a normal man insane,
A grown, cheerful man can start the day with a smile,
Then begin to tie his turban and after a while,
He's locked in mortal combat with demons and ghouls,
Cursing God and the Heavens, calling the saints fools,
Ready to beat his dog and leave his wife.

Kurtas became *cholas*, and long became in,
We wore boots to our hemlines, women and men.
Towering turbans were tied lower over the years
And waistlines expanded as prosperity appeared.
We wheeled and dealed as we hustled and faked it
And one-upped each other, trying to make it
Through the balance and imbalance of life.

We've learned to work with each other, if not together,
Something we're still learning and it could take forever
But, one thing is clear; we won't get there alone
For, only through our unity will the way be shown.
And even then we'll argue if it's the right way
And whether we should move by night or by day
And who should ride in front and who behind.

We agree to disagree and we disagree a lot.
We agree they are wrong; they disagree, they're not.
I disagree, but then I usually do
And if you agree with me, I'll disagree with you,
Not for its own sake, I don't mean to disagree,
Though I might be in denial but then, I guess that's me.
Mostly, someone is wrong is what I find.

As I fight with my turban I study my face,
Where there used to be brown, now there's white in its place,
Where I used to be trim, now what I find is a waist,
Where I used to be fast, now I move with less haste.
The conclusion draws itself, though the job is not yet done,
And still, I am grateful that together we are One,
And that it's not out of place to be real.

Espanola, New Mexico
10 January, 1996

27

KEEPING UP

"Keep the lines straight," was what he said.
"Face your partner and cover your head.
Hold the hands and keep the spine straight,
Look deep into the eyes to make yourself great!
Keep up! Keep up! Keep up! Keep up!

"Hold, be strong and let the energy flow,
This time God has given for you to grow.
Hold your partner tight and chant *Wahe Guru!*
And please don't let go, whatever you do!
Keep up! Keep up! Keep up! Keep up!"

For two and a half hours we sat in those lines,
Raising our voices and straightening our spines,
For six hours a day we blew our minds,
Changing our destiny by changing the Times!
Keep up! Keep Up! Keep Up! Keep Up!

Bananas and oranges and potato soup
Came as breakfast for the whole group,
For dinner were lettuce, beans and rice,
We hid our carrots but the hot sauce was nice.
And we Kept Up! Kept Up! Kept Up!

By the third day people began to freak,
Husbands and wives would fight, but not speak,
We sneaked from the camp to get something to eat,
But each new day he would again repeat,
"Keep Up! Keep Up! Keep Up! Keep Up!"

For eight long days we tried our best
To get through it all, avoiding the test,
But none were immune, so all were blest,
And by the end we had reached the crest!
For we Kept Up! Kept Up! Kept Up!

Then we would dance, and spin, and sing
Into the night, the mountains would ring!
Though some would cry and others would scream,
We had raised the banner to fulfill the dream!
Now, Keep Up! Keep Up! Keep Up! Keep Up!

Espanola, New Mexico
10 January, 1995

THE PRICE

If we had known all those years ago
What it would take to make us grow,
Chances are we would have never begun
To walk this path to the Infinite One.

But many hearts heard Destiny's call
And many have come and given all.
Though many could not stand the test,
Many tried and gave their best.

But there were those of malignant heart
Who tried to tear our unity apart,
Who believed this Khalsa is not True,
Who betrayed the Trust of their Guru.

In the Gurdwaras they wouldn't accept us,
At Ross Street they wanted to hurt us,
By them we shall never be accepted,
But we are grateful to have been rejected.

They are Sikhs and they shall die in shame,
But we are Khalsa and so shall we remain!
They shall be forgotten, they won't expand,
But *Takhat a Khalsa* shall continue to stand!

So it fell upon us to pay the price,
To bear the weight and sacrifice;
To lay the foundation upon this land
Then transform the consciousness of Man.

We carry with us the disappointment and pain,
And the deep frustration of loss and gain;
Of people leaving and promises broken,
Of trust betrayed and falsehood spoken.

For this is the gift of God to Man:
The power to Love, but not understand
The depth of the Heart or height of the Soul,
So we must bow low to maintain control.

If we had known all those years ago
How high we could rise, how far we could go,
Chances are we would have never refused
To do our sadhana and pay our dues.

Espanola, New Mexico
15 June, 1994

THE SPARK

There was a time, some may remember,
When the spirit in us was like an ember
And at that time, some may recall,
We began to rise and answer the call.

There was a point, some began to know,
When the ember in us had begun to glow.
It spread through us, to our delight,
For that glowing ember was Guru's Light!

For twenty-five years, some might suggest,
The ember was fanned by challenge and test
And fueled by sacrifice, surrender and pain,
It has caught the heart and burst into flame!

The Children of the Cusp, we might be called,
Have started a fire that can't be controlled.
Blown from the Heavens by the Winds of Change,
The Consciousness of Man it will rearrange.

But let us remember that once we were dark,
Then hammer and chisel ignited that spark,
And that humble artist who put blade to stone,
Walks through the Flames to sleep in the Dome.

Espanola, New Mexico
17 August, 1994

TO BE A TEACHER

In early August of Nineteen Seventy One,
After a year in the Ashram and college was done,
I was told that Memphis had taken a dive
And that I should go to keep it alive.
So, with a sleeping bag and one suitcase,
I set my course to pursue the chase
To my Greatness.

I was young and full of dreams,
With no experience of what Life means,
A fantasy dreamer, full of fear and doubt,
With only five dollars when I started out,
But despite all that, I did have Faith,
Which was well-tested when I got a taste
Of Life's bitterness.

I believed I was a teacher; that the time had come
To pursue my Destiny and leave my home.
So the Greyhound took me North, then West,
And when I arrived, I faced my first test.
"No one here does Kundalini Yoga anymore.
There's another path we prefer to explore,
To find our way."

Another teacher had done his thing,
And my first three classes, nobody came,
But each evening I walked five miles to the Park
Where I would teach my class, just before dark,
Of one or two, sometimes even four or five,
And with those few dollars I could survive
From day to day.

I could not find a job with a turban and beard
For there in the South it was extremely weird.
I wasn't a hippie, but I was still a freak,
Though people liked me because I was unique.
Then in September I turned twenty-one,
So officially my adulthood had begun,
As I began to grow.

In a halfway house was where I stayed;
To maintain order over those who strayed
Into that place, usually late at night,
Wanting to crash, though some wanted to fight.
And many came who had OD'ed on dope,
Or who had run away because they couldn't cope
And had nowhere to go.

I lived on cabbage, yogurt and beans,
Which kept me healthy, sexy and lean,
And from four to eight, with each day's dawn,
I did my sadhana, which carried me along
Through those times, when my life was changing,
For each new day I was rearranging
My heart and mind.

I worked as a laborer at a construction site,
And I would teach my classes every night.
Then, in the halfway house I learned about life
From the shattered people who had come through strife;
To ask for help, for food, or a place to sleep,
All those long ago memories now I keep
In my heart and mind.

And in many cities across this land
Other young teachers tried their hand,
For each one lifted and carried forth the Flame,
Yet, there are only a few who still remain,
Who rose to the challenge of Guru's ways.
We struggled together through those early days,
So long ago.

It all seemed so hard way back then,
But at times I think back and remember when
I taught those tiny classes in that Park
To those few people, sitting in the dark.
I feel happy and grateful to my Guru
For those simple tests that He put me through,
To make me grow.

Espanola, New Mexico
4 January, 1995

A FEW STEPS
ON THE
PATH

ONCE AGAIN

One more round we've walked together,
One more chance to touch a heart,
One step closer we've come to Forever;
To carve the Destiny before we part.
For now, once again, through Grit and Grace,
Commitment has conquered Time and Space.

Once again we've stood the test,
Once again we've held on tight,
Once again we've done our best
To keep the Grace and the Light.
Now we turn to walk the round again,
A few last steps before our suffering ends.

We do not walk this path alone
Despite this isolation,
We walk together to be as One
As we lead our Khalsa Nation.
We sacrificed for something Great,
We seized Destiny, conquering Fate.

All our Family is with us now,
All our joy is around us,
All together let us bow,
While Guru's Love surrounds us,
It is Guru's Love that binds us
And His wheel that Shines us.

Someday soon we both shall sleep,
When Guru takes us in his arms,
But our Sacred Family He shall keep
And watch them grow, safe from harm.
For once again, through Grit and Grace,
Love has conquered Time and Space.

Espanola, New Mexico
22 November, 1994

37

BABA

There, beneath the arch, recessed into the wall,
Unflinching in winter's cold, you sit without a shawl,
Immune to summer's heat or autumn's cleansing rain,
Consistent as the sky or an ancient hymn's refrain.

You take no shelter from the sleepless eye of the sun,
Sitting still beneath the moon, you focus on the One,
In that profound immersion and ever in control,
You probe the depths of the heart, to touch the Sacred Soul.

Silently you meditate, in your solitary trance,
And spin with the Devas and the Demons your stationary
dance,
But to we who walk this earth and never see you move,
Comes a sense of awe and wonder, absolute as Love.

Though we should not disturb you, you're available if we call,
In extreme life or death, or if honor is about to fall,
It only takes one request (it's an insult to ask again),
And though you never move, you always prevail and win.

Personally I am grateful for all the help you have given me,
The inspiration for meditation and the flow of my poetry,
Though you remain immovable as the wall, silent as the night,
You are always there to help us, and ensure that we get it right!

Between Pittsburgh and Albuquerque
2 September, 1996

THE OAK CREEK BRIDGE

In the heat of June we drove all day,
Across the desert, down Arizona way.
The deep blue sky and the dancing heat
Had me mesmerized, though I fought off sleep.
The road twisted beneath the bright pink ridge
Then into madness, across the Oak Creek Bridge.

The has-been's, the prophets and the never was
Were there in the Name of the New Age cause,
With their beads and crystals, staffs and rings,
We met many former Kaurs and Singhs,
We met the psychics and shamans galore,
Who told us the stories of ancient lore.

We went to the places where the Indians prayed,
We saw the developments the white man made,
We stood on a mesa and listened to the air
And learned that many come to meditate there,
They are driven in jeeps by guides who are lost,
Who have by Time, been spun and tossed.

We visited a house that once was a barge,
And was crammed full of junk, though not very large.
In the evening was class, attended by few,
Perhaps all the shamans already knew
The sacred science that comes through Grace,
Which frees us from the bonds of Time and Space.

We heard about this trip and how powerful it is,
We learned about that trip, taught by a whiz,
So much window-shopping and so few goods,
So many souls seemingly lost in the woods.
We felt like aliens from a far away star
So, after two days we got back in the car.

In the car we were silent as we passed the gate,
We left in the dust those who might have been great,
For the energy that comes down must be reflected,
Not absorbed, inverted, or by fantasy projected.
Then, I understood how sharp is Guru's Edge
As we drove away, across the Oak Creek Bridge.

Espanola, New Mexico
9 August, 1995

COMMITMENT

Commitment is the Answer!
Commitment is the Life!
Commitment is the Lover,
Commitment is the Wife!

Without Commitment
Love would be lost,
Commitment is the payment,
And commitment the cost.

Love is the power
That makes Saints of men,
Commitment is the reason
The Saints never bend.

Duty is my Sovereign,
Dharma my Banner,
Meditation my Origin,
And Sadhana my Hammer.

Life is for growing,
God is for loving,
Love is for knowing
Commitment is the Answer!

Rome, Italy
December, 1989

THE CONVERSATION
A True Story

I was asked today by a younger friend,
"Do you think this complacency will ever end?"
"What complacency is that?" I replied.
"The growing spiritual complacency," he sighed.
"Spiritual complacency, what do you mean?"
"You older folks have grown complacent, it seems."

I squirmed in my seat and averted my eyes,
Should I hear him out, or should I deny?
Is this for real, is he telling the truth?
Must be the innocent delusion of youth,
We're the pioneers of the Aquarian Age!
Our story is written on destiny's page!

Trying to sound mature, with a lump in my throat,
(I supposed this boy was meant to rock the boat),
I asked him to explain what he had said,
Was there still hope or were we spiritually dead?
What complacency could there possibly be,
What was I blind to that he could see?

"Well, to my generation, you guys are getting old.
It's like, 'Don't do as we do, do as you're told.'
I mean, some go to sadhana, though usually late,
And sometimes at night, I think a few meditate,
But it is more than practice; it's a state of mind,
And you guys seem so sluggish and falling behind.

"We don't see your light, not even a spark.
I don't mean to say that you're all cold and dark.
But you know, when we were little a spirit was there
That now, when we look, seems to have vanished in air.
I'll tell you, more often than not what we see,
You stay at home and eat and just watch T.V.

"I mean, the experience of consciousness, I believe,
Is the purpose of Dharma and how we should live,
But I don't see that happening, none of us do,
So we are unmotivated to follow things through.
We believe you're sincere and want to be great,
I don't mean to say that I think it's too late."

I sucked in my breath and asked my heart to slow down,
I sat there in silence, not making a sound,
Then he dropped a mega-bomb from out of the void,
"It seems you have all become what you wanted to avoid.
I mean, you have tried and most have done their best,
But you guys have to get past this one last test."

This is a true story that I am sharing with you,
Which struck to my heart like a bolt from the blue,
Perhaps it is just the sweet rebellion of youth,
Only we can decide if he was telling the truth,
Yet, somehow I think that something is there,
I only speak for myself, though this story I share.

Let us look in our hearts and meditate deep,
There is too much at stake, too much to keep,
Too much to be lost, if this boy spoke true;
This sacred trust, which was given by the Guru,
It begins within, in each sincere heart,
It can be changed; we have only to start.

Espanola, New Mexico
28 August, 1995

DIETS

Fifteen cloves a day you can eat,
With a glass of orange juice to make it sweet;
Five in the morning and five at lunch,
With five in the evening to complete the bunch.

It cleanses the blood, the bowels and the lungs
And cleanses false friends, when they turn and run.
It rejuvenates the cells and your eyes will shine bright,
But keep the door open when you sleep at night.

Bananas are a most magnificent fruit,
Which grow high on the tree, not at the root,
Three times a day, three bananas you consume,
Between the times of the new and full moon.

But that's not all and what follows is nice,
For the next forty days eat mung beans and rice
Which, by the way, is the best diet you see,
For it's a total food that digests easily.

The "P" diet is fun and easy to keep,
Only foods that begin with "P" you can eat,
Pizza, pasta, pancakes and pudding are out,
Fruits, nuts and vegetables are all that count.

Potent potatoes proceed with a "P,"
But this diet is followed separately,
Beets are good for kidneys and liver,
Have them each day and you'll live forever.

Eat and enjoy, but when you eat, be wise,
For your stomach is smaller than your eyes
And before you eat, there's one thing you must do:
Give thanks to the One who gave it to you.

Espanola, New Mexico
19 September, 1994

GOD WAITS ON THE STEPS

Each morning they come to the Gurdwara door,
Their bright eyes shining in the electric lights,
While together they pass the last of the night,
Bringing joy to each one who enters to pray,
They honor the sangat by night and by day
And with their tails, they sweep the floor.

Patiently they wait as they peer through the glass.
Longing to enter, yet they seem to know, not this time.
With devotion they come, quieter than the children who whine,
Humble as we should be, grateful for whatever they receive,
And with a simple nuzzle or lick, our tensions they relieve.
Then with gratitude they take prasad from all who pass.

Each Sunday morning they arrive before me,
Humbly they wait with reverence at the door,
They ask only for a pat or prasad, nothing more.
I could learn a lot from their devotion,
For their humility fills me with emotion,
It is unequaled here by any who I see.

Though they don't really speak, they have a lot to say.
They observe us come and go, passing out and in,
They have watched us grow, watched us struggle and win,
Watched us suffer and laugh and cry through loss and gain,
They are always with us, sharing our joy and pain
And I always miss them, whenever I'm away.

Vancouver, Canada
18 March, 1996

DOUBT

I have traveled far and wide,
I have meditated long and deep,
Yet still in me there is a side
That fails to open, which darkness keeps.

I have probed myself in and out,
And tried to do what seemed right,
But in my mind there still is doubt,
And darkness where there should be Light.

What great wrong have I done
That I fail to push on through?
Why is Victory's song unsung?
Why do I doubt you, my Guru?

What service have I failed to render,
What sacrifice have I failed to make?
How can I find my way to surrender
That in me, which you will not take?

How much longer to be fulfilled,
When daily there seems to be no gain?
What sacrifice, what strength of will
Can help to ease my constant pain?

Is it asking too much to See?
Have I failed to do enough?
How much older must I be
Before you find me good enough?

I call your Name into the Night,
I meditate in the cold and dark,
What sweet Prayer must I recite,
That I may see you in my heart?

How can I stop from playing the role
Of living with this Dark Attitude?
What stain must be washed from my Soul,
So that I may live with Gratitude?

It is only Gratitude that will Change
Me from darkness into Light,
Only your Grace can rearrange
My tarnished Soul to one that's Bright!

So, hear this doubtful prayer of mine
And open that which remains shut,
That Gratitude should fill my Mind
And break the shell of this tough Nut!

Espanola, New Mexico
26 April, 1994

YOUR FACE

Though I cannot see your face, I always feel your gaze,
Nor have I seen the hand, which has held me all my days,
I cannot see the breath, which comes without a thought,
Which forms the sacred fire wherein true grit is wrought,
Illumining the chambers of the mind where destiny is sought,
When your light comes shining brightly through the haze.

Though I cannot see the cold, I can feel it upon my skin,
As it penetrates through my shawl when driven by the wind,
I feel it upon my face, whichever way I turn,
Though I cannot see the wind I can feel the air churn,
Though I don't recall the subject, the lesson I must learn,
Or you will call me before the judge once again.

And through this fog of Maya I see many blinking lights,
Each one more inviting, promising refuge from the night,
And though I long to stop and enter that warm and cozy space,
Where I can lay my head to rest without cold upon my face,
Something pulls my sleeve and sets me again at a steady pace.
It is your Grace, which I can't see, though I am ever in your sights.

Though I never see your hug, I always feel your squeeze,
I know when you are angry, but seldom when you're pleased,
I know when you are listening, but I don't hear you when you
speak,
Perhaps because I'm complaining, or perhaps because I'm weak,
Or perhaps because with these nine holes I always spring a leak.
Yet, you're always there to plug me, and put my mind at ease.

Espanola, New Mexico
1 October, 1996

48

GURU'S GATE

Where you enter below that humble arch,
Is not the place to haggle or shop,
It is the Gate through which the soldiers march,
The place where all cowardice must stop,
For *Ek Ong Kar* is inscribed at the top.

It swings only one-way: in, not out
And though heavy, for wrought with steel,
With a gentle push it will swing about,
Opening onto the path that's real,
The path we walk, so the Soul may heal.

The path slopes down to a more humble place,
Past Baba Siri Chand in his meditation deep,
Silently he sits in that profound space,
Beyond the fringe of the quantum leap,
For that sleepless vigil is his to keep.

The white gate stands open, though it will latch,
It is secure, but it will not lock,
For the treasure within no thief can snatch,
For those who shall have it, no one can block,
And to receive it you have only to knock.

The Gate of the Guru is open for all,
The destination of the path is the same,
For to each Divine Soul who answers the Call,
Is bestowed the gift of the One God's Name,
Set alight by the Shabd Guru's flame.

Espanola, New Mexico
10 June, 1996

WITH GRATITUDE

We are grateful they turned us away,
When starry-eyed and naive we came
Innocently, to Guru's door to pray
And be with those who recited the Name.

We are grateful they refused to teach us
When we asked, with sincerity to learn,
We are grateful they refused to help us,
For that which we've learned, we've earned.

We are grateful that they turned us out,
And threatened us with sticks and words,
For the seeds required manure to sprout,
Now, those sticks have been parried with swords.

We are grateful that Guru's kindness
Has put us through such a challenging test,
And we are grateful that through their blindness
They have created such a miserable mess.

We are grateful that out of desperation
We built Gurdwaras that are beautiful and clean,
Homes for our Sovereign Spiritual Nation
Which shine on brightly with dignity's sheen.

We are grateful that the Age is turning
As the clash and controversy begin to fade,
And the prayer of the immortal soul's yearning
Is realized by the foundation we've laid.

We are grateful that we stand together
Without gender, or color, or race;
Under our flags, which will fly forever,
For Victory is the gift of Guru's Grace.

Los Angeles, California
21 May, 1996

50

THE MESSAGE

He told us back in 1969,
"Get ready now, it will soon be time
To heal the people and ease their pain,
Many will come, though few will remain.
Many more will carry the weight."

He told us again in '71,
"Prepare yourself for those who will come;
For those without hope, broken and lost,
Who have fallen and stumbled, been spun and tossed,
Who have plummeted from the height.

"Come not as disciples, come only to teach,
This is your destiny and the goal you must reach,
We will walk there together; take each other's hand,
We will build a new consciousness upon this land,
Which will stand for thousands of years."

For all these years the message hasn't changed,
Though many have left, there are many who remain,
Many who have stood up and shouldered the weight,
Though we might be remembered as those who were great,
We are just the Freaks of the New Frontier.

We walk now with honor, we live now in Grace,
We have kept up and grown up and carved out our place.
But the message remains, like the gong his words ring,
"Hail Guru Ram Das and Heal the World!" we sing.
And as ten times greater let our heads touch his feet.

Los Angeles, California
11 April, 1996

51

PROSPERITY

It eludes us like God Himself,
Or so it sometimes seems.
We think it is fulfillment of the Self
And the fulfillment of our dreams.

It is the gauge that we regard
As the measure of the Man,
Without it life can be truly hard
When money is our only stand.

But, consciousness is not measured
In gold, or coins, or cash,
It is the heart that should be treasured
And valued for it's cache.

For let us be realistic
And not fail to understand,
That money is not caustic,
But the actions of the man.

Why prosperity eludes us
Only Guru can explain,
Only when it includes us
Can we find relief from our pain.

It's in the heart that poverty begins,
Then the spirit it devours,
And many with wealth are bankrupt within
And many poor, die bitter and sour.

Prosperity is the song of the soul
And the expansiveness of the heart;
The living identity of one who is whole
With himself, with God in his heart.

Together let us celebrate and share
The prosperity that binds us together,
The gift of Dharma and Guru's care,
May his banner fly unfurled, forever!

Espanola, New Mexico
15 August, 1994

MY PRAYER

"Let my mind find confidence," is the way I start my prayer,
"Let my soul find peace and keep it ever in Thy care,
Let me find my life's purpose, so that I achieve my best,
Let me live my life with gratitude," this is my one request.

"Thank you for this kriya, that has changed the course I walk,
Thank you for my teacher who made me do it, instead of balk,
Thank you for the opportunity to practice it here, today,
And thank you for the simple desire to do it in the right way.

"Bless my beautiful teacher, who for this mission has given his heart,
Grant that he will see us as ten times greater before he departs,
Grant to him Your protection and heal him through and through,
So that he can complete his mission and return back Home to You.

"Grant that I can serve him and hold his sacred trust,
And carry his banner forward, high above the dust,
Let Your light shine through me, clear and radiant and bright,
And grant that all I touch may have the experience of Your light.

"Bless my beautiful son, keep him safe, secure and strong,
And kick him in the head if he takes a turn that's wrong,
Bless the soul of my daughter, keep her safe forever,
Thank you for the blessing of our brief, sweet time together.

"Bless my beloved Sadhana, always cover her with Thy Hand,
Hold her tight, though sweetly, when we're in separate lands,
Guide her to her destiny so that she can understand her place,
Grant that she finds her fulfillment and always keeps her Grace.

"Bless Akal Security and each one of them who has served,
Grant that all will be blessed and receive what they deserve,
Grant that undying, Akal will continue to stand,
And free me of this karma someday soon, if you can.

"Bless this beautiful family that all will find their joy,
Bless our beautiful children, every innocent girl and boy,
And help all those who through sickness of body, heart or mind
Have lost their hope and joy and wander, lost and blind.

"Thank you for this prayer, Oh Lord, and the gift of the True Guru,
Guru is the main thing that reflects most well on you,
Please cover my faults and fill in for all the rest,
I would be deeply grateful, and I am sure you would be blessed."

Espanola, New Mexico
2 August, 1995

MY PROBLEM

Now, I have a certain problem, perhaps you have it, too,
It has plagued me all my life, affecting everything I do,
As far back as I can remember, in fact, ever since my birth,
I can't seem to accept the fact that I'm here on planet Earth!

I have tried not to accept it, but it is always in my face,
And I know if I don't correct it, I'll be stuck here in this place,
The one thing that I know, and on this Truth you can bet,
The Universe isn't likely to change just because I'm upset.

Oh, I have talked to God and have spoken rather well,
I have asked His explanation, but He doesn't have much to tell,
Because all He is *Is,* and He does little more than prevail,
Though He has moved me through this life at the pace of a
crippled snail.

I mean, I don't want to seem ungrateful, in fact I don't mind,
Because whatever test He gives me is not meant to be unkind,
Though sometimes His sense of humor is a little out of line,
Then all He does is smile and say that everything is fine.

Now the Earth is a great place to visit, I've come many times
before,
But each time I've had trouble leaving and getting out that door,
In fact, many tours I've taken, mostly with the same guide,
And every time he's told me, "You're not just along for the ride."

Well, I've prayed at every shrine and tightly held my breath
And waited for that moment, though I'm not intrigued by death,
And I don't mind telling you the challenges have not been small,
But the worst part of my problem is I can't accept I'm here at all.

Some day I'll get on top of it, some day I'll get it down,
"Keep up", is what he says, "it'll soon all come around,"
So that is what I do and actually, it's an enjoyable way to fake it,
And somehow in my heart, I truly believe I'm gonna make it.

Los Angeles, California
21 February, 1997

55

LIKE A ROCK

I have dressed myself in bana, radiant and white,
I have washed, oiled my beard and tied my turban tight,
I bow before the Guru and lay my dollar down,
But in my mind through the kirtan, I hear a different sound,
For there is something in there that I can't yet control,
Oh, my Lord, please help me 'cause I still love rock 'n roll.

I have met the saints; I've even met the Pope,
I have talked with sages, though I find little hope,
I have perfected the five kriyas, but still in my mind
Loud guitars and electric sounds are often what I find,
I gently hold my mala and through my fingers feel each bead roll,
Oh, my Lord, please help me 'cause I still love rock 'n roll.

I have studied and practiced so I can recite my banis,
Kirtan touches me deeply and I love to hear the ragis,
The focus of my life is my disciplined meditation,
I believe in spirituality and a lifetime of devotion,
I love to sit in silence and listen to the song of my soul,
But, Oh Lord, please help me 'cause I still love rock 'n roll.

Often when I'm driving, various shabads I recite,
Or other spiritual songs usually fill me with delight,
But I have a major problem that shows me that I'm weak,
For it doesn't take very long before I begin to fall asleep,
So, only to avoid an accident do I let the good times roll,
Oh, my Lord, please help me 'cause I still love rock 'n roll.

I don't know where I've failed to get my mind set right,
But there dwells in me an urge that I am unable to fight,
What can I do to stop it, how can I change my style?
Perhaps I should play polkas or country for a while,
I only pray sincerely that I haven't stained my soul,
Oh, my Lord please help me 'cause I still love rock 'n roll.

Espanola, New Mexico
16 January, 1995

SADHANA

Deep in the night, before the day
When warm and peacefully I lay,
The time comes to challenge death,
To leave my bed and take the breath
Deep into my sacred space.

I face the dark before the light,
I face the challenge and the fight,
I face the fear, the anger and pain,
I face the past yet call again
Deep into my sacred space.

The madness crashes 'round my brain,
My anger rushes like a train,
My frustration rises like the sea,
Still the japa propels me
Deeper into my sacred space.

Passion's fire burns hot and bright,
As the day burns away the night,
The steam of lust, the grip of greed
Surge in me like a charging steed
And still I feel my sacred space.

In the cesspool of my mind
Are graphic thoughts of acts unkind,
My fantasy life must be fulfilled,
Yet as I breathe my mind is stilled,
Resting in my sacred space.

In my brain creeps the fog of sleep,
Clouding my mind with sights unique,
The chill of morning pushes me deep
Into my shawl where it's not really sleep;
Only my sacred space.

The mudra falls into my lap,
Perhaps it's time to take a nap,
I meditate a lot anyway
And there's a lot to do today!
Anywhere is my sacred space.

Someday it will make me great
To sit in the dark and meditate;
Late at night and before the day
When I could sleep, or dream or stray
Away from my sacred space.

Still the breath comes and goes,
And through the day the mantra flows,
And in my heart I feel a song,
(Though sometimes the words are wrong),
And that *is* my sacred space.

Espanola, New Mexico
30 March, 1994

SCENES FROM A MARRIAGE

I. A Momentary Lapse of Reason

With tears in his eyes he loudly cried out,
"She's my soul mate and God, how I love her!
This is the right thing I have no doubt,
I only love her and no other!"

Without raising his voice the master spoke,
"But, what about your children and wife?
Do you mean to abandon them without hope,
Tarnishing your reputation and your life?"

"This marriage is wrong, it can't be right,
Because she is the only one who I Love.
They'll recover and be all right,
But this angel was sent from above!"

"You think you have found the woman of your dreams,
And that this will bring fulfillment to your life,
But I must tell you, my son, to me it seems
That you are falling upon your own knife."

"But how can that be, this love is so strong,
And my feelings are so real and alive !"
"Trust me, my boy, your feelings are wrong,
Look past them to the Truth that's inside.

"Feeling is feeling and dealing is dealing,
And you must deal with what you feel, like a man,
But this fantasy life will leave you screaming,
Let her go, you must recover while you can."

"Then I will always hold her in my heart,
But I will go back and do what I should."
"Thank you, my son, you've made a good start.
Simply, let your heart tick and pump the blood."

II. Pearls in the Swine

This guy is useless, that's what I see,
He eats, he sleeps, he watches TV,
He can't make money or do anything right,
He stinks, he's loud and he snores at night.
He sleeps through sadhana, he hates his job,
He's too overweight and looks like a slob.

Why can't he be spiritual like, well, you know who?
Why can't he be successful and more like you?
Why should I try to inspire this stone?
Why should I nurture a meatless bone?

If he were only stronger,
If he could just be great,
If he could just *last* a little longer,
If his spine were strong and straight.

When we were young we had inspiration,
When we were young we dared to dream,
We felt we were one with God's creation,
That we were woven into His flawless seam.

He used to laugh and meditate,
He used to teach and inspire,
Somewhere in him is something great,
But, can I re-ignite his fire?

I saw it once, way back then,
Let me try to find it, again.

III. Happily Ever After

The telephone rings: "The call's for you,
You're late for duty and the rent is due,
You're off again, you're never home,
And you leave me here all alone."

"My clothes need ironing, dinner is late,
The way you treat me, I'll never be great,
I've got to work, that keeps us alive,
Then you lay your insecurity jive?"

"You're insensitive!"
"Well, you're insane!"
"You're ridiculous!"
"Then, you're to blame!"

"A man never stumbles unless
The woman he's with makes a mess!
The woman is the cause of all
The cracks that cause the fall!"

"The woman holds steady if the man
Keeps the dignity when he stands,
And holds his identity, come what may,
Even when conflict comes his way."

"All right then, maybe I slipped,
Maybe I stumbled, or was I tripped?
Let's try again, it's all we can do,
Although I don't say it, I do love you."

"That's because you have a head like a stone!"
"Such is the power of testosterone!"

IV. Toward a Deeper Understanding

Together in the dark, once again we try
For an intimate moment, just you and I,
Then the telephone rings or the children cry
And the moment is lost, like smoke in the sky,
So we turn and roll over.

And I find myself thinking
As I lay here, limp and cold,
That our lives go by racing,
And I feel I'm getting old,
That I've turned and rolled over.

In the dark I feel you turn
Ever so slightly to the right,
Then I hear your breath return,
Such a miracle in the night!
And my mind turns and rolls over.

And I remember that day I walked with you
Four times around the Siri Guru,
And I think about how far we've walked,
How much we've said, how little we've talked,
How much we've turned and how much we've rolled over.

It's caused me to grow, caused me to cry,
Taught me to sacrifice; to say *We*, not *I*.
I once was a boy, now I'm a man
And despite it all, I'd do it again.
Now I turn, close my eyes, and roll over.

Espanola, New Mexico
12 December, 1994

SIMRAN

You came to us upon the mists of the night,
As you lifted each heart, giving it flight
Over the jagged mountains of the mind,
Caressing each soft soul, making it shine
With the radiance of Thy shimmering light;
Farther and farther, into the deep Blue,
Dying each fiber of Self with Thy hue,
So there was no distinction of me or You.

Simran is the caress of Guru's Grace
That closes the mind and touches the Heart,
Which removes the Self beyond Time and Space
For there, through surrender, True love will start.
And softly, in the still darkness of the night,
Each sweet heart and kind soul was shining bright!

Los Angeles, California
14 April, 1996

ST. VALENTINE'S DAY

The time of the heart is Valentine,
But feelings and emotions make us blind,
The lovers ask, "Will you be mine?"
At this time called Valentine.

Yet in the heart this Love's harpoon
Rips a deep, unhealing wound,
The lovers cry like hounds at the moon,
Such is the pain of Love's harpoon.

I know this pain that makes us crawl,
I know the tragedy of the fall,
Yet when my back was against the wall,
Guru Ram Das heard my call.

Then you, my Master, by Guru's Grace,
Healed my wound and saved my face,
And with Thy instruction I found my place;
Such is the power of Guru's Grace.

What I would suggest, if I could,
Is that the heart just pumps the blood;
That the commotions become like wood,
I would suggest this, if I could.

So at this time called Valentine
My feelings are to be Divine.
I ask you, Master, "Make me Thine,"
At this time called Valentine.

Rome, Italy
14 February 1990

THE THRESHOLD OF ZERO

How much closer to Zero, how far away from the Whole?
How many times must I bow down and wash the root of my Soul,
So I can live this life as One?
How far away from You must I be, before I cannot bear the pain?
How many dips in Thy Nectar Tank are required to remove the
Stain,
For this dirty job to be done?

I hover here around Zero, though I long to be at One.
How to eradicate my everything so that Zero can be won,
Then I can experience my birth?
Why do I fail to release my grip, I desperately hold on tight,
So that total Zero eludes me and I cannot see Thy Light?
Then, I am bound here to this Earth.

I still cling to the Illusion, unable to cross that Line
That will take me into Zero, so that you can fill my mind,
Then this Lifetime can begin.
Yet, I race around the circle, I meditate, bow and pray,
Still I am unable to surrender and like an ass, I bray
For You to come and let me in.

The door stands there open; no one is turned away,
I awake each morning hoping, that this will be the day
That I enter your Sacred Space.
I've put my forehead to the threshold, then run away like a thief,
I've cried into the darkness and been blinded by my grief,
Unable to take my place.

How far away from Zero, how far away from my Soul,
Before I let go of everything, until I can be Whole
And merge into the One?
Zero is there before me; the way in is marked and clear,
There is no secret or mystery, no need for grief or fear,
No need to turn and run.

Actually, it is quite simple, this drama is just for show,
To cover my procrastination from walking where I must go
And getting the job done right.
Commitment is the answer and gratitude shows the way.
My Guru walks before me, guiding me day to day,
And covering me through the night.

If each day I make a commitment unto my regal Soul,
With an attitude of gratitude, which ever keeps me whole
And which frees me from my pain,
Then I will bear with Grace whatever is given to me,
Instructing my foolish mind not to grumble uselessly,
Or, with drama whine in vain.

And when at the Threshold of Zero I touch that Sacred Place,
If I hesitate to enter in, with confusion upon my face
Unable to enter through that door;
Please, hear this simple prayer from this melancholy man,
And overlook the griping, that's not really what I am,
Then bless the forehead on that floor.

Vancouver, Canada
14 March, 1996

FROM TIME TO TIME

The radiant, ancient Age turned Silver from Gold,
Leaving the Truth three-quarters of old,
Then the Silver darkened into the Copper Age,
When Truth was half of that original page.
And Copper hardened into the Age of Steel,
Where one-quarter Truth turns the Eternal Wheel,
This is the Age of Iron, the Age of the Machine,
Where Truth is lost to fantasy and dream.

The Civilizations of those enlightened times
Have returned to the mud in now desolated climes,
This is the power of the Immortal Lord
Who created this World because He was lonely and bored,
There is no longer a trace of the Golden Age,
Though that story can be told by every sage,
Those shining days of Silver have turned to dust,
Lost to the Akasha, under the blue Earth's crust.

The Age of Copper faded and left no trace,
Lost to the blind justice of Time and Space,
Leaving us here now, in the quarter Truth's light,
Dim to the masses, but to the few it shines bright,
It is an Age of Darkness for those sentenced to Fate,
But an opportunity for those who can relate
To the power of the Shabd, which will guide us through,
For Kali Yuga is the Age of the True Guru.

This is the Age of Enigma, the Age of Change,
The Age of Incarnations, wonderful and strange;
When the chance to grow at an accelerated pace
Is there for the brave soul who enters the race,
Animal souls have incarnated in human form,
Humans behaving as animals, has become the norm,
It is the Age of Technology, which will make you insane,
And the only salvation is to recite the Name.

It is the Golden Age, in this Age of Steel,
When before the Truth, Mankind must kneel,
The last tick of the clock before we fade to black,
Then into the Eternal, all things will flow back,
To start the endless cycle once again,
From the Age of Gold to the Age of Sin,
Yet through the darkness of the gathering night
There shines the brightness of Guru's Light.

From our tempered steel will shine golden rays,
To guide the children of those future days
Through the Age of Darkness, by that flashing spark;
Struck when chisel meets stone, illumining the dark.
And the mark of the Master who dropped hammer to blade
Will remain through the Ages; it can never fade.
For, it is only struck upon that heart which is true,
And I think if you look, you'll find it beating in you.

Los Angeles, California
13 January, 1997

TODAY

I had a painful thought today,
Of those who were taken away;
Who had trust that was betrayed
By those they loved.

Today I felt a pain inside
For those little ones who cried
When they were turned aside,
By those they loved.

Today tears came to my eyes
For those sweet and innocent lives;
The little ones who heard lies
From those they loved.

Today I felt deep despair
For every soft lock of hair
Which was cut without a care,
By those they loved.

Today I had to weep
For the sorrow that I keep
For them, small and sweet,
Betrayed by those they loved.

Today I felt deep shame
That I could not ease the pain
Of them who can't remain
With those they love.

Espanola, New Mexico
16 March, 1994

A QUIET TRIUMPH

I experienced a quiet triumph today,
When the Amrit Vela came my way,
For I was very tired late last night,
But my REM's were short in flight,
For an old black dog gave the Rebel Yell,
Then my neurotic cat began raising hell,
Stealing my precious sleep.

Then at 3:15 the music played,
So I turned it off, but in bed I stayed
A little longer, stretching the night,
Wishing to sleep, but engaged in a fight
Between my funk and my caliber and grit,
Sleep was so sweet but I was in a fit
That only I could control.

So at 4:00 I found the floor
And staggered, in a daze, to the door
Then across the hall to wash and brush,
While all the world rested in a hush
Of ambrosial air, sweet and cool,
As I stumbled around like a doddering fool
Splashing absently in a shoal.

My ablutions done, I fumbled around
And found my skin, then laid it down,
Around my shoulders I pulled my shawl,
I folded my hands and began to call
On the One Creator and transparent Guru;
To tune me in and guide me through,
So I could meditate deep.

Sidh Karm Kriya is what I do,
So hands in the trident, a deep breath I drew,
And focused the energy and recited the sound,
But I kept moving and squirming around,
Yet I kept up, though not that well,
Then in my lap the mudra fell
As I began to fight off sleep.

However great a man may be
Sleep usually claims the victory,
So in the dark I started to fight,
As day began to overcome the night,
Like a noodle my spine went limp,
But I fought hard not to be a wimp,
For 2 -1/2 hours was my goal.

The thing about combat that is known by few;
You are never unscathed, whatever you do,
And though I tried, sleep got in her blows,
As I twitched and nodded and fought for control.
For two hours I struggled as sleep tightened her grip,
Then, as the sky grew light, through her noose I slipped.
Now, I was on a roll.

For the last half hour my form was great,
Like an ancient yogi or blossoming saint.
Then I understood where the triumph lay,
For my sadhana was the victor today,
I had only taken a simple short step,
Then Guru crossed that open gap.
Now, that experience is mine to keep.

Espanola, New Mexico
24 July, 1995

A FEW HARSH WORDS

There's a crack there, in the mirror,
The reflection is fractured and unclear,
The view of Self is distorted,
The voice of reason you've failed to hear,
For that crack was there before.

The mirror keeps the reflection
As you once kept the Trust,
The view of Self is distorted
And you can't face it, though you must,
Or die from your own self-rejection.

Each little sliver, though broken
Reflects back to you the whole,
And the view of Self is distorted,
Refracting the light of your Soul,
For the Truth must always be spoken.

When you follow the line of the crack,
What is the cause that you see?
That the view of Self became distorted
And shattered your harmony,
Causing you to take a step back?

The great vision of God is your destiny
And to achieve it you walk this course,
The view of Self must be mended,
You must dive in and know your source
And shine in your radiant dignity.

There is no blame on the outside,
For the struggle is fought within,
The view of Self must be mended,
You must get up and start again
And understand there is no free ride.

It is time now, to grow in your Glory,
It is time now to live in your Grace,
Let the view of Self be exalted,
That Honor may shine on your face,
For that is the rest of the story.

Between Espanola & Houston
13 January, 1996

THE YO-YO

I am Your yo-yo, and up and down I spin,
I rise up to the top, then roll and fall again,
I dangle on Your string, spinning in the air,
Until You pull me up with patient, loving care
And hold me in Your hand until the spinning stops,
Then, Your fingers open up, and once again I drop.

Always on Your finger, I dangle by a string,
While spinning at high velocity causes me to sing,
You send me 'round the world or walk me on the ground,
You launch me through the air, then pull me up without a
sound.
Ever in control, I follow what is Your will,
But all this up and down sometimes makes me ill.

Yet You hold me in Your hand, standing over all,
Although You let me drop, You never let me fall,
You never let the string break, however wild I spin,
And when I'm out of control, You always pull me in,
And hold me in Your palm as Your fingers pull the string
Then, once again You release me, quickly, with a fling!

Around my shining core Your unbreakable string is wound
And to Your Infinite Will this simple soul is bound,
I am balanced between Your fingers and off their tips I roll
And I pass the ride more smoothly when I don't fight You for
control
Because, when I fight You, the string gets knotted and slack
Then, I lose momentum and it's much harder to get back.

So send me 'round the world, rock the cradle, walk the dog,
Fly me through the sunshine or fly me through the fog,
Spin me at high velocity or spin me slow and free,
Let me hesitate at the bottom or bring me up with glee,
But please don't let me go, please hold me with Your string,
For if it ever breaks, I'll fall with a thud, not a ring.

Espanola, New Mexico
11 January, 1995

74

THE HAND
OF THE
GURU

WHERE THE SUN SETS

In the crystal silence of ice and snow,
Echoed through the peaks and the lake below,
Sat a rishi with long, coiled hair,
The song of Heaven frozen in the air.

God himself sang that song,
The rishi silent, his breathing long,
Then God spoke upon the frozen air
To the rishi with the long, coiled hair.

"Oh great rishi, I've a need for you,
An important job that only you can do."
The rishi, still, spoke not a word,
But said, in silence, "Do it yourself, Lord."

The Lord answered, laughed out loud,
"Oh great rishi, you make Me proud!
But this job must be done by hand,
It doesn't require God, it requires a man."

"Through all the Ages, to ease Man's pain,
Many I have sent in my Name,
Krishna, Buddha, Jesu and Rasul
Did the job and gave the tools."

"Sadly though, it is My great pain
That only the personality remains.
It is these cults of personality
That keep Man's soul from being free."

"I need you now to bear the Sword
That Man may bow only to the Word,
You must go to end this tyranny
And 960,000,000 you shall be!"

The rishi spoke, "Then let's agree,
I will go but You'll work *through* me,
I'll do this job, but make no claim,
So only there will be You to blame."

God, in His Mercy, smiled and said,
"Then all who come must give their head.
This sacred Khalsa that we'll create,
Shall be in every land and state."

"And when the New Age comes,
Look to the place of the setting sun,
There shall burn my shining Light
As the Day burns away the Night."

Rishi Dusht Dhaman held his breath,
Then transformed himself, cheating Death,
He flew like a hawk, through the Spiritual Sky
And took the birth as Gobind Rai.

He created the Khalsa to reign supreme
And by them was made Guru Gobind Singh.
The Siri Guru he set in place,
To give us guidance through Time and Space.

And in this land of the setting sun
The Age of Aquarius has begun
To fan the ember of Guru's Light;
Into a flame that is burning bright.

Espanola, New Mexico
14 March, 1994

THE WEAVER OF DESTINY

For twenty-seven years in that tiny room,
In secret solitude you probed the heart,
To join the pieces that were broken apart,
Like a weaver sitting before a loom.

You drew the spindle and pulled the thread,
Weaving the tapestry of Time and Space
With the thread of the Guru tightly in place,
Then to seal it, you gave your head.

Did it take all those years of meditation
For Rishi Dusht Dhaman to agree to try
To take the birth as Gobind Rai,
So there would stand our Khalsa nation?

They came to you, desperate and broken.
Without hope they came before the Guru,
To ask for direction on what to do,
Then those words, by Gobind, were spoken.

Were you proud as a Father, when he spoke,
To know that he had understood the Call,
That he was prepared to sacrifice All?
Were you relieved that now there was Hope?

Was it painful for you to ride away
From that sweet, shining boy of invincible heart?
Were there tears in your eyes when you turned to depart?
Was there a part of you that longed to stay?

When there, at Delhi, in the Red Fort you were kept,
They demanded miracles to save your lives,
And Bhai Mati Das was tortured before your eyes,
Was there ever a time, in your heart, when you wept?

Bhai Mati Das argued that you should leave,
Then offered to die so the Dharma could survive,
As he recited Sukhmani, he was sawed alive,
Were they shocked by what a Sikh could achieve?

Then came the morning when they gave you the call.
Two times before they called you to appear,
And you stood before them, but showed no fear.
"Produce a miracle or your head will fall!"

"The One God is the Miracle you don't see."
Then you took the paper and wrote the note,
And placed it in the locket before you spoke,
"Why don't you come and worship Him with me?"

You recited Japji, then bowed with Grace,
Then the great sword fell and cut off your head,
And when they opened the locket your note read,
"The miracle is, I gave my head, not my Faith!"

Three hundred years later, where the sun sets,
Do we have that grit to face the saw,
To die with honor before we fall,
To stand fast, however painful it gets?

Oh Weaver of Destiny, Liberator of Lives,
At the loom of the soul you have woven your thread
Into the tapestry that is We, and through heart and head
You have sealed it, in each of our Lives.

Espanola, New Mexico
28 Sept, 1994

GURU OF MIRACLES

The streets of Goindwal, You walked alone,
Selling Your pulses to stay alive,
A simple orphan trying to survive,
Then Guru called You into His home.
And You, afraid and insecure,
Began to cry because You were unsure
If this experience You would survive.

But Guru, in His mercy, took You in;
And Bibi Bani He made Your wife
To inspire You through Your trials of life,
But there was still more for You to win.
So He raised and tested and hammered You,
He found Your heart pure, then crowned You Guru
And You cut through Maya's veil like a knife.

Three sons were born through darkness and light.
Though Prithi Chand's deception betrayed Your trust
And You were forced to dismiss him with disgust,
Still, there was Arjan, your heart's delight.
His longing for the Guru, sweet and pure,
Was fulfilled when You set Your signature,
For the Guruship to Him, did You entrust.

You gave to the world the Sarovar
To wash away the wounds of the Soul,
Where we who are broken are restored, whole,
And those who are defeated start over.
Then in it the Harimander was placed,
Where all who bow are touched by Thy Grace
And those who have longings are consoled.

To guide us in marriage, You wrote Lavan.
To give us direction and see us through,
Our lives should orbit around the Guru,
And in our Souls, two hearts should beat as One.
For it is in the cozy home that God is found,
Where Grace and Dignity and Love abound,
Where life itself can be renewed.

Your Beloved Son came and bowed at Your door
And prayed that You take his powers away,
That his ego should fly and His soul be saved,
Then nightly for four years, He washed Your floor.
But Guru's prophecy was to be fulfilled
So, You sent that Son with the iron will;
To carry Your banner and show the way.

And here, in the West, a few were found
Who learned of the Miracle of the Fourth Guru,
Who laid the foundation upon which we grew,
It is here that Your praises resound.
Many lives have been touched by Your hand,
And by Thy Grace we continue to expand
And our hearts You continue to imbue.

Oh Guru of Miracles, before You we pray;
That we should remember, when lost and dark,
Our way is illumined by Guru's mark
And through You we will find the way.
For this is the Miracle of the Fourth Guru,
That You hold our course, straight and true,
And Your Son, the Yogi, has chiseled that spark.

Espanola, New Mexico
23 October, 1994

STOCKHOLM

I had done the job and paid the price,
But failed the test, though it saved my life.
So I spent three months in European towns,
To recover myself and settle down.

One day in September, about mid-day,
Through the streets of Stockholm I made my way,
When I found an ancient church standing there,
So I slipped inside for a moment of prayer.

The sounds of an organ, mellow and deep,
Drew me further inside, so I took a seat.
My mind, by the music, was mesmerized,
So I focused myself and closed my eyes.

My breathing slowed, became deep and long,
While the sounds of the organ carried me along,
Then breath-by-breath, I left that place
And found myself in a deeper space.

I had a vision of the 5th Guru
On a plate of iron, with a reddish hue.
Below the iron were searing flames,
But the Guru, still, did not complain.

Upon his head they poured red-hot sand,
Yet Guru Arjan never raised a hand,
But before Him stood Mian Mir,
The Sufi Saint who Guru held dear.

With tears in his eyes and quivering voice
He cried, "Oh, Guru, You have a choice!
You don't have to endure this torture and pain,
Use Your powers and put out these flames!"

Guru smiled and His parched lips cracked,
The burning sand rolled down His back,
In a weak, soft voice that I could barely hear,
He said, "I cannot do that, Mian Mir."

Mian Mir sobbed in anger and pain,
"Oh, my Guru, there will be no shame,
If You prove that God's Power and Grace
Surpasses these fools *and* Time and Space!"

"If you feel that You cannot act,
Then let me try, I'll break their back!
I cannot stand here and watch You die
Without helping; *please* let me try!"

Guru serenely sat on top of those flames,
"Oh, Mian Mir, please let Me explain:
I don't do this to prove that God is Great,
I only do it so My Sikhs will meditate."

With effort He smiled and softly said,
"It doesn't matter if I'm alive or dead,
If my Sikhs prefer powers to God's Name,
Then truly I shall have suffered in vain."

"My Beloved Friend, meditate with Me,
Sit straight, close your eyes, and you shall see
The reality I experience here and now,
The One True power before which we bow."

Reluctantly, Mian Mir closed his eyes,
Then smiled to himself in sweet surprise,
For on a mound of snow Guru sat,
With snowflakes falling, keeping Him wet.

Mian Mir bowed before the Guru
And with tears in his eyes, slowly withdrew,
But before he was gone, Guru softly said,
"The Truth is in your Heart, not your Head."

The sounds of the organ hung in the air
And movement in the church made me aware
That I could not sit there and drift and float,
For I was in Stockholm, waiting for a boat.

That vision I saw, so deep and intense,
Was not a lost dream but a living experience,
I was there with the Guru and Mian Mir
And as I write these words, they are with me here.

"The Truth is in your Heart, not your Head,"
That was what Guru Arjan had said.
Truth is the Power before which we bow,
It was the message then, and it's still True now.

Albuquerque, New Mexico
7 September, 1994

AMRIT, IN THE AMRIT VELA

Today you touched us, once again,
Before the dawn of day began
To spread His soft light in morning's sky,
To light the clouds and close the eye
Of the stars and sliver of the moon.

They bowed their heads as they faced the sword,
For they had come in grace, to give their word;
To face the challenge and take their stand
And walk your street with head in hand,
Then they stepped into that room.

The water was poured into the iron bowl,
The five Piaras maintained control,
The sugar was added to make it sweet,
Then, slowly the khanda began to sweep
Through the water, to make it strong.

Then, your banis they began to recite,
As day emerged from the cover of night,
The sound of the khanda, constant like a drone,
Sparked each heart, through breath and bone,
As each mind listened to your song.

Then one by one, they took their place,
To accept the Nectar, by Thy Grace,
Five times they sipped it, five times in the eyes,
Five times at the crown, where the ego dies,
The Five K's they wore, to be like you.

This sacred form shall remain unchanged,
Not hair, nor skin shall be rearranged,
The Rehit shall be followed, to keep us straight,
Guru mantra we recite, to make us great
And we bow only before the Siri Guru.

Then you spread your Grace to all who were there,
For the remaining Amrit we were able to share
With all the sangat, who came to bow low,
As one by one we sipped from the bowl
And our hearts filled with delight.

As the chill of the morning began to fade
To the light of the Sun, which chased the shade
Behind the rocks and under the trees,
The depth of Your love was easy to see
In those smiling faces, shining bright!

Espanola, New Mexico
17 July, 1995

THE PRAYER OF THE ANGELS

Eighty four lakhs of angels were there,
When Guru called for a brave man's head.
Each one who stood, they blessed with care
And over them all their wings were spread,
While before the Guru they offered their prayer.

The Piaras he transformed and restored them whole,
Radiant and bright before the sangat they stood,
The angels bowed with reverence to each divine soul
Who had faced the sword and spilled his blood,
While Guru stirred the Amrit in the iron bowl.

They knelt with devotion, as the angels cried,
And received the Amrit, by Guru's Grace,
He smiled to those who had run to hide
And called them back from their hiding place,
For in all his children he takes great pride.

Before the Piaras he bowed his head
And asked that they give the Amrit to him,
"Khalsa is my True Guru," he humbly said,
And tears filled the eyes of each one of them,
Who beneath his steel had sacrificed and bled.

Then those who had turned and run away
Returned and bowed before the Five,
They asked the Guru if there was a way
They could redeem themselves, while still alive,
"You can accept this Amrit here, today."

Thousands came forward on that sacred day,
To receive the Amrit and take a vow;
That they would ever walk in Guru's way,
And before no man would they bend or bow,
Or from this path they would never stray.

Then, before the Guru the angels came
And bowing to him with folded wings,
They prayed for the Amrit and gift of the Name,
So that they could become Kaurs and Singhs;
That in the company of the holy they would remain.

With a smile from his Heart, upon his shining face,
Guru lovingly blessed them with a humble bow,
"The time will come when you will take your place
In my beloved Khalsa, but that time is not now,
For the will of God must unfold at it's own pace.

"Someday in the future the day will come,
When the word of the Guru has crossed the sea,
Then, in that distant land of the setting sun,
I will call for you to come and be with me
And together, we will stand and be as one."

The hub of the wheel of the New Age has turned
And the angels are descending to claim their birth,
To extinguish the fires of madness, which have burned
Throughout the Ages upon this tired Earth,
This is the incarnation their souls have earned.

Those angels are sitting among us today
And more will come in answer to their prayer,
To carry forth the banner of Guru's way,
So that all Mankind will be made aware,
That the Age of the Guru is here to stay!

Espanola, New Mexico
27 July, 1995

ANOTHER LIFE,
ANOTHER CHANCE

We, who sat in the dust that day,
When You stood before us, Sword in Hand,
Who fought the urge to run away,
But failed to find the courage to stand:
Is this our second chance, today?

We who came and demanded to go
From Anandpur Sahib, that sacred place;
We, those fools who could not bow low,
Have another chance to find Thy Grace.
Will we see You, again, bend Your Bow?

Like a Hawk, You came from the Spiritual Sky
And with Your Love, You claimed us as Your own,
Against the fools You let Your arrows fly,
You became our Father and gave us a home.
Is this our second chance to die?

Do we give our heads when we keep the Kesh?
When we wear the Kirpan, do we keep Thy Grace?
When we wear the Kacheras, do we remain Chaste?
Does the Kanga keep our Kundal in place?
Does the Kara remind us to avoid Disgrace?

Oh, Lord of the Sword, Master of the Heart,
Oh, Shining Saint and Victorious Warrior,
This form You have given is the Highest Art,
Grant that we see You each day in the mirror,
For, today You have given us a new start!

Espanola, New Mexico
Baisakhi, 1995

BAISAKHI DAY, TODAY

If you were standing there today,
Ringing steel flashing through the sky,
Would I turn and run away,
Or stand and take the chance to die?

If, today, I heard your call,
Bleeding steel above your head,
Could I bow and let it fall,
Then carry it and move ahead?

Could I bend to touch that place
Where life as we know it, ends?
Then carry on without a trace
Of what I, before, had been?

If you took your flashing steel
And probed the depths of my heart,
Would you find the contents real,
Worthy to stand and take the part?

Between the Ages, in the Cusp,
What kind of saint-soldiers are we?
Can we uphold the Guru's Trust
To keep our Grace and Dignity?

Can we keep alive the Call
You gave upon that Northern Plain,
Prepared to die before we fall,
Despite the losses and the pain?

On that day, when with sword you stood,
The call was loud, the enemy clear,
Your signature was written in blood
And holds sacred our honor here.

But what of those who in this time
Betray the Khalsa for their own gain?
Can they continue to lead the blind
Into a life of grief and shame?

This, your Khalsa, which is your life,
Shall stand, despite who comes or goes.
For it is in the face of strife
That we find, in ourselves, the foes.

If you were standing there today,
Ringing steel flashing through the sky,
I could but choose the Khalsa Way,
For there is no better way to die!

Espanola, New Mexico
Baisakhi, 1994

91

A FLASH OF BLUE

Sometimes, *there!* I catch them,
Just in the corner of my eye,
With sword and shield and lance,
In a sweeping arc they dance
Untraceable, like wind in the sky,
Yet always there around me.

Sometimes I notice them on horses
Following wherever I go,
Patiently they wait in camp,
Immune to the cold and damp
Or the softness of the snow.
They wait or follow silently.

Sometimes I hear the creech and clink
Of steel and leather and wood,
When together they move with me
Quietly alert, though patiently,
I would feed them if I could,
But in silent vigil they wait.

Sometimes through my window
I sense movement in the dark,
Against the deep blue of midnight,
Movement beyond my line of sight
Turns my head with a start,
Then fades again to dark.

Sometimes in the early morning
Before light crosses the peaks,
Before night's purple shadows
Abscond across the meadows,
I sense them, yet they don't speak,
For the sacred trust they keep.

Perhaps it is my imagination
That perceives that flash of blue,
Perhaps it is only my longing
For a deeper sense of belonging;
Yet others have seen them, too.
Perhaps then, so have you.

Espanola, New Mexico
18 January, 1996

ALL MY CHILDREN

We had plumbed the lines and dug the troughs,
And laid the rebar, so it would be strong enough,
The conduits were in and the forms were set,
But when the concrete came, it was much too wet.

We had to shovel and nurse it all day,
We had to push so the forms would stay,
The October sun and the bright blue sky,
Watched us work and kept our spirits high.

The day wore on and began to fade,
But by the end we had set the grade,
The sun pitched down and headed West,
The foundation was set and we felt blessed.

My back ached and my fingers were sore,
But I had worked on that historic pour,
Takhat a Khalsa had laid down its roots,
So I staggered home and took off my boots.

I was dirty and tired with a spinning head,
So I skipped the shower and laid on my bed
And closed my eyes, but I didn't fall asleep,
I fell into a trance, my breathing long and deep.

I felt lighter than my body, lighter than air,
And I began to rise up, leaving it there
On the bed, as I drifted away in the night,
Then I found myself standing back at the site.

The work we had done was still there in the ground,
But from behind my right shoulder I heard a sound
Of horses hooves and someone calling my name,
A loud, startling sound, which I could not explain.

A magnificent warrior then rode into view,
I knew when I saw Him, it was the 10th Guru,
He turned in the saddle, then tilted His head,
"I have come for All My Children!" He said.

With sword held high, He rode away into the night,
With a great rush of wind and a thousand points of light,
I gasped with excitement, my heart raced in my breast,
For the Guru and Neela had ridden away to the West.

And here, now, in Takhat a Khalsa we sit,
Humble and cozy, though the roof leaks a bit,
And I understand now that His words ring true,
For *we* are the children of the 10th Guru.

Espanola, New Mexico
14 September, 1994

TO: *Siri Simran Kaur, Sr. -- Personal Secretary to Yogi Bhajan*
FROM: *Gurutej Singh*
DATE: *6 March, 1996*
RE: *Report on Recent Tour*

ENGLAND TOUR

Trailing, twisting, sonic screaming
Through the night, our engines gleaming,
We crossed the Pond and at morning's light,
Upon British soil we ended our flight.

February's gloom, cast down grey,
While through London towne we made our way,
The Master sat in the four-wheel drive,
With Randir at the wheel to keep him alive.

At Ravenshaw, behind the green door,
We walked upon that sticky floor,
Cat hairs filled our noses and eyes,
While Miri and Piri barked and cried.

Two hours later, to our great relief,
The luggage arrived, every piece,
While the Siri Singh Sahib, safe from harm,
Took a long, sweet nap in Guru's arms.

We talked, we laughed, we sipped our tea
And as the day wore on, it was plain to see
That we weren't going anywhere that day;
That he was settled in and intended to stay.

St. Valentine's Day broke sunny and bright,
(Though soon the clouds obscured the light),
He was out the door in a blinding flash,
And to Navleen's house he made his dash.

With the Jethadar he pondered things great,
While the rest of us talked or slept and ate,
Then the sun pitched down from its heavenly abode,
And the time had come to hit the road.

Randir drove like a bat out 'a Hell,
As I followed along (rather well),
To the Midlands, along the Motorway,
In a stumbling procession we made our way.

In Birmingham it was cold and dark
When we finally stopped and were able to park,
We unloaded the bags (through the paint fumes).
Then the jetha left to sing their tunes.

Guru Har Rai Gurdwara is where he spoke
To those confused and clueless folk,
Though some were friendly and wanted to know
How to ease their pain and how to grow.

Then back at the house he talked into the night,
Filling us all with joy and delight,
Then saying good night, he climbed the stairs
And we went to sleep (after braiding our hair).

In that house with one bathroom,
Eleven slept in various rooms,
So, in the morning I crossed the street,
To wake Randir from his sleep.

He, or someone would let me in
So my morning ablutions could begin,
It was usually another who opened the door,
While Randir continued to snore.

He saw many people throughout the day,
Then Thursday night we made our way
Back to Gurdwara Guru Har Rai,
Where the Jethadar spoke with twinkling eye.

The Siri Singh Sahib spoke for a short while,
Then the Jethadar began to play with a smile,
But kirtan didn't cover what he wanted to say,
So he started with katha, to our dismay.

He droned on and we began to fade,
Not understanding a single point he made,
But that night was not the only treat:
He did it the next night, in stifling heat.

So, we ran around for a day or two,
We saw the factory and how to make shoes,
We ate saag and stayed up late,
Though Dharma could sleep in any state.

Then Sunday morning was bright and clear
As we drove to South Hampton, full of cheer,
But to make a stop was a growing desire,
When Randir's car blew a tire.

It took some time to make the switch,
While the SSS waited with an itch,
Then at one-hundred per we headed South,
Which caused me to drive with open mouth.

South Hampton, from where the Titanic sailed,
Was cold and grey and for awhile it hailed
As we arrived beneath the old stone steeple,
Where he spoke to fewer than a hundred people.

Then back behind the wheel and into the race
To Birmingham at a breakneck pace,
Where two programs we did that night,
Doing the job and doing it right.

Monday we split and some stayed behind
To continue the quest for heart and mind,
But with the Siri Singh Sahib we headed down,
Through the cold and grey, to London towne.

First was a meeting where they laughed and yelled
While we waited around, hungry as hell,
Then off to Navleen's where we foraged a snack,
Then to Barking, we launched the attack.

It was snowing, now, but we didn't slow down
And through the streets of London our way we wound,
From the Barking Gurdwara to Regent Park,
For the meditation course he had to start.

In less than an hour he did the job well,
Then back to Barking we drove, pell mell,
For a late night meeting with you know who,
But we left again, before the tea could brew.

It was late when we reached Ravenshaw Street,
So he climbed the stairs and went to sleep,
But we set out to make our way through the night,
To our place of rest, but we got lost outright.

There were many students the next day to see,
So at the ashram we dined on TVP,
Then, into the traffic, through those narrow streets
And up to Birmingham, a program to meet.

We did two programs on Tuesday night,
But at langar we noticed something not right,
For in that house all was not as it seemed,
When we were served langar by raging queens.

They served us the langar from steaming pots,
(Though they desperately needed hormone shots),
While in falsetto voices they primped and swished
(To get out of there was our only wish).

Wednesday morning we left in frenzied haste,
And down to Reading on the Motorway we raced
Like bullets, along the highway we flew,
Then my left front tire suddenly blew.

Across the highway I careened and veered,
Because with no front tire it was hard to steer,
The deflated rubber was chewed and burned
When onto the shoulder I finally turned.

The other cars disappeared ahead,
While Siri Ved and I, glad we wern't dead,
Changed the tire, which was no small feat,
Then set out again, the Triple S to meet.

The Reading langar was the best by far,
Then once again it was back in the car
For the race back North, to meet with the youth,
Where the Siri Singh Sahib told them the Truth.

Then another Gurdwara and langar again
Served by the flaming Bobsey twins,
Who called themselves sisters, that was a twist,
Then around one a.m., we drove home in the mist.

Thursday they came throughout the day,
To visit the Master and learn his way,
Or to get healed or freed from their pain,
Then at night, to the Gurdwara again.

Friday we had lunch at the home of some Sardar,
Who very carefully had hidden his bar,
Then, we drove to London as day surrendered to night,
And at Singh Sahaba Gurdwara, he shed his light.

Saturday, to Barking we drove for lunch,
(There must have been twenty in the whole bunch),
Then to someone's house where, to our surprise,
She looked at another with ardor in her eyes.

After South Hall where he gave them the Word,
We had a birthday party at the Standard,
That ended the day, late once more,
But Sunday was the last day of the tour.

Eight programs we did in a row,
After they played, the Jetha would go
To the next location where he was to speak,
Then he would follow, tired but not weak.

The two youth programs we did that day,
Revealed a generation looking for a way
To have the experience that will make it real,
To give them something they can know and feel.

The Sikhs of England seemed lost and dark,
There is a faint glow, though mostly a spark,
But among the youth there is some hope,
If they can avoid sex and dope.

They want what we have but they seem afraid
To walk this path which Guru has laid,
They want our help, they want to learn,
But they don't understand that it must be earned.

The tour was successful, the Jethadar was pleased,
The Siri Singh Sahib put his mind at ease,
We are truly grateful to our host, Randir,
But I would advise him to be careful with Balbir.

So, Monday morning we loaded the van
And drove through the traffic, following the plan
And at Heathrow airport we said our goodbyes,
Then made our way home through the azure skies.

Espanola, New Mexico
6 March, 1996

TO MY FATHER, WITH GRATITUDE

Oh, my Father,
You walked with us that day.
I felt You as I looked out
From that hill where You stood,
Dripping, ringing steel in Your hand.

I felt You there when I saw those Shastrs
Which had been held by You, the Shakti
Still alive in them, almost *shimmering!*
So alive! Like the breath that comes out and in.
So real! Like the destiny we share together.

I imagined Your voice in the drum
That morning, when I sat with my Master
And we bowed together at that Sacred place.
Mostly, though, I felt joy and laughter
From deep within the memory of my soul
And I thought of You standing there, laughing.

I tasted Your prasad, *now it is in me.*
I tasted Your langar, *now it is part of me.*
I breathed the air You breathed and
My pranas were charged by Your spirit!
How can I feel fear when You are with me?
How can I feel depressed when You are with me?
How can I not be brave when You have led the way?
Take this head, it is useless on these shoulders.

When I sit with the sangat, do I feel You?
When there are five of us together, do we know You?
When I look in the mirror, do I see You?
You *are* there, always, real and alive!
You have answered my prayer, and I am grateful.

Espanola, New Mexico
12 March, 1995

THE MECHANIC

When in the cylinder of Pisces, deep within your mind,
The acceleration of Aquarius begins to heat and grind
The piston of the psyche, until it glows and burns,
Then your God-tuned engine seizes and it no longer turns,
So the oil of madness leaks out and stains you through and through,
Then the only mechanic who can repair you is the *Shabd Guru*.

When the wheels of the personality are unbalanced and unaligned,
So that you drift across the lanes that your Destiny has defined
And you find yourself in a ditch along this course of Grace,
With your axels bent and broken and mud upon your face;
Then the calibrated instruments that set you straight and true
Are applied by the Divine mechanic we call the *Shabd Guru*.

When our emotions turn inside us and our passions rock and knock
And we blow smoke from our tailpipes, dirty, black and hot,
And our environments get polluted by the exhaust we cannot burn,
Then we breathe the toxic gasses that cause the Soul to return,
Sadhana is the valve-job that keeps your smoke from turning blue,
And the only mechanic who can repair us is the *Shabd Guru*.

When the antenna of awareness gets disconnected from the mind
Then, because of static, a clear channel you cannot find
And the sounds of anger and depression play loudly in your head,
Then the flow of Life has ended, for you are neither alive nor dead.
So, to catch the tunes, you know what 'cha gotta do,
Head for that Circuit City that we call the *Shabd Guru*.

When your lights have finally dimmed and you're almost out of gas
And with breathless acceleration, you make that last attempt to pass,
If you hold on to the wheel and focus on the sound
As you race along life's highway, with the accelerator down,
When you come to pay the toll, if you keep on driving through,
Know that you won't get caught, for you've been fixed by the *Shabd Guru!*

Los Angeles, California
20 April, 1995

THE SACRIFICE

It was a time for death, to be transformed
It was a time for pain, when many mourned,
It was a time for sorrow, loss and strife,
A time for suffering and sacrifice,
So on the 6th of June, 1984
The tanks rolled over that marble floor,
And the Akal Takht laid itself down.

These Times, so strange, required so great a price,
That the Akal Takht, *itself,* made the sacrifice,
And as the cannon roared and the rockets flared,
As bullet bit bone and flesh and blood and hair
Spilled across that Parkarma, turning it dark and red,
While in the sarover floated the bodies of the dead,
The Akal Takht laid itself down.

The youth of a nation were lost that dark night,
When compassion and reason had taken flight,
When God, in His mystery moved His Great hand
And death and sorrow claimed that ancient land.
The tanks rolled on, over marble and blood,
Firing their rockets where ever they would,
And the Akal Takht laid itself down.

And by that command the Dynasty fell,
For by their own hand was struck the knell
Of death and the changing of the Ages,
As Truth shall appear on History's pages;
To tell the story of deception and lies,
And heartless men, who ignored those cries,
When the Akal Takht laid itself down.

All that was Sacred was put to the test,
All who sacrificed, by Guru were blessed,
They killed all they could and tortured the rest,
But the spirit stood strong, bringing out the best.
For, no sacrifice is ever made in vain
And that memory is carried, by we who remain,
Of when the Akal Takht laid itself down.

Espanola, New Mexico
7 Aug, 1995

THE VICTORY

After you're gone and we're on our own
Will we stand as One or stand alone?
Are we able to carry this load so great
That only together we can bear the weight?

Will we find the way to inspire ourselves
Or fall away into our private hells?
Will we fight for power, lust and greed
Or will we continue to spread the seed?

And what of those young and innocent lives,
The blondies and angries who have no guides,
Will we take them and guide them through,
Or will we allow them to leave their Guru?

Will we stand together that no one may fall
Or will we stand for ourselves, ignoring the Call?
Will those who are weak be covered and saved
Or will the vultures upon them prey?

Who will tell us to rise and stand
If we are unable to lift a hand?
Will our Gurdwaras be hollow and dark
Or will they glow with Guru's spark?

If we fail now to find our place,
How can we survive Time and Space?
If each other we cannot inspire,
We will loose our spirit, like air from a tire.

We will flatten and fatten and no longer roll,
We will have lost our spirit and our soul,
But if Guru's ember in even one of us lights,
The flame will catch and keep burning bright!

Let us light the heart now, so the head will bow,
Let us Pledge ourselves and to each other vow,
That we'll stand together for all to see
That Victory comes only through unity.

Espanola, New Mexico
8 August, 1994

IN
GURU'S
FOOTSTEPS

WE'RE GOING!

My heart quickens and my head feels light,
Butterflies in my stomach have taken flight,
My breast rises, then I laugh with delight,
I lie in my bed but I can't sleep at night,
I can't concentrate, I can't read or write,
But ever so soon I will be all right,
For I'm going to the Golden Temple again!

I feel excited, awake and alive!
Senses and emotions are on overdrive,
I must remain focused, now I must strive
To contain myself so that I can survive
The remaining weeks before I arrive
On that cold Parkarma, where I will revive.
I'm going to the Golden Temple again!

I remember the first time I touched that place,
When I walked that Parkarma at the master's pace,
With tears in my eyes, golden air on my face,
I tasted the sweet Nectar of Guru's Grace,
And though I lost all sense of Time and Space,
I felt at home, for I had touched my base,
Now, I'm going to the Golden Temple again!

The sound of the music, the shade of the light
Permeate the Heart so the Soul shines bright,
And in the cold water where the fishes bite
The debt of your karmas you can requite,
If you dip down deep, you will reach the height,
Then the Flame of Love's passion you will ignite,
I'm going to the Golden Temple again!

Let's join together in a humble prayer,
That Guru will protect us while we're there,
That all will be well and under His care
While we are apart, between here and there,
And let each one who goes carry the prayer
Of those who remain here, while we are there,
We're going to the Golden Temple again!

Espanola, New Mexico
11 January, 1995

HARIMANDER, IN THE AMRIT VELA

The dark of the morning had gently begun
Pushing back the night to make way for the Sun,
The wetness of the marble and the cold of the night
Filled me with joy and my heart beat with delight!
I walked with the Master, his hand on my arm,
With the Love of the Guru keeping us warm.

The sounds of the kirtan hung in the air
While in the trees, the birds recited their prayer,
"Quickly, bring the prasad," I heard him say,
Then he released my arm and I skidded away.
I slipped toward the counter (not wanting to be late)
For a hundred rupees of prasad, which filled the steel plate.

With the treasure in my hand, my feet moved fast,
I touched forehead to marble, then through the gate I passed,
I gave my receipts to the sevadar (he counted them all),
Then I scurried and slipped forward, trying not to fall,
I quickly crossed the bridge, moving through the crowd,
Then stopped before the door and at the threshold I bowed.

I crossed the threshold and stepped into the Light,
Then handed the prasad to the sevadar on my right,
I bowed to the Manji, where Guru would soon sit,
Then went around to the back and took a quick sip,
I moved to the side and looked through the door,
But there was nowhere to sit on that crowded floor.

Safely he sat in that space, so tight,
He was covered securely to the left and right
So, I sat outside, my back to the rail,
And for a few peaceful moments, let my mind sail.
The strains of the kirtan and the hum of the crowd
Played the morning raga, with my head in the clouds.

Then something happened that I can't quite explain,
For through the crowd and the kirtan, I was hearing my name,
I opened my eyes and looked all around
But I couldn't identify the source of the sound,
So I closed my eyes and lowered my chin,
But, before I was set, I heard it again.

Softly, like water flowing over stones,
Guru was calling, welcoming me home,
I felt joy in my soul and was almost overcome,
When straight through it all came the sound of the drum!
Powerful and strong, challenging the night,
It awakened the morning to Guru's light.

Soon there was movement and the sound of the horn
And a rush to the palanquin on which Guru was borne,
I rose to my feet, my heart raced in my breast,
And moved to the Guru for the chance to be blest,
I moved through the crowd, Guru was coming straight,
Then slipped under the rail and shouldered the weight.

Only a few, brief steps were all I was allowed,
Then someone stepped in and I merged with the crowd,
The sound of the bugle continued to blow
As the voices of the sangat continued to grow,
I returned to my place as Guru entered in
And gave thanks to be on that cold marble again.

Espanola, New Mexico
5 March, 1995

BANGLA SAHIB

The steps were wet, the marble cold,
As I walked through lifetimes of prayer,
The dark morning sky over this place, so old,
Held the vibrations, which hung in the air.

We climbed to the top while the music played
As my withering mind gave way to my heart,
In my hands a garland and prashad, just made,
Seemed like treasures and sacred works of art.

The lights from inside glowed yellow and bright,
Then I looked up and saw light on the dome,
And deep in my heart day broke from night,
I had awakened and found my way home.

And off to the right where a few people stood,
They were pouring water into the pilgrim's hands,
They sipped it and splashed it, the bad and the good,
For Guru's mercy falls, like the rain, on all lands.

We walked to that place where Guru once sat
And lovingly took on Himself the plague,
For thousands of people were saved by that
Sacrifice for them and the coming Age.

The water, cold, fell into my palms
And trickled down my throat and face,
While below, children begged for alms,
As the morning light began to fill the space.

As we started to walk in I heard him say,
Like a voice that fell, softly, from the sky,
"This water heals people, even today,"
Then I choked and started to cry.

And I understood within myself
The depth of Guru's love for us all,
That sweet little boy, who sacrificed Himself,
Simply listened and answered the call.

For many days after when I would recall
That moment, when with my teacher I stood,
I would begin to cry and my tears would fall,
But I felt grateful and happy and good.

That water heals people, even today,
But it springs from the heart, not the ground,
For it is when we walk in Guru's way,
That the source and the stream are found.

Espanola, New Mexico
31 August, 1994

THE FISHES

Upon the marble, warm and white,
We walked together every night,
While the Harimander, covered in Light,
Was reflected in the water, shining bright,
And we bowed together with delight.

Upon the Parkarma the pilgrims slept,
In Guru's hand their prayers were kept,
There were many who smiled, a few who wept,
And with joy and devotion each heart leapt,
As we walked the Parkarma, step by step.

The Dukh Bhanjan Tree was there,
Over the Parkarma in that humid air,
And under that tree he stepped with care
Into the shimmering, holy water where
The fishes came, his darshan to share.

In the dark water we could see them splash
While, upon their backs the bright lights flashed,
All their fishy karmas turned to ash,
As they swam to him, their prayers to cash,
It was a joyful, though reverent bash.

Their open mouths gaped large in the dark,
Those old souls, whose prayer was to mark
Themselves with the light of Guru's arc
So, in the sarover they struck the spark
Of Guru's love in that divine park.

Each night they came as never before,
Coming two by two and four by four,
They pointed the way to Guru's door,
Then, from the water, they bowed to the shore
As his wet feet touched that marble floor.

Then into the water they dived down deep,
To pray to the Guru, their souls to keep,
While on the Parkarma was heard not a peep...
Well, except for a snore or a birdie's cheep,
So, we returned to the Mohan and went to sleep.

This is the power of the saintly man,
Whom God shall cover with His own Hand,
The four corners shall bow to where he stands,
In all of the regions, on all of the lands,
So, practice his wisdom, whenever you can.

Espanola, New Mexico
31 October, 1995

GOINDWAL

Where the land lies green on fertile ground,
At the bend of the river, Goindwal is found,
In this humble village lived three Gurus:
Amar Das and Ram Das, and Arjan, too.

At the bottom of the eighty-four steps
The pilgrims go to take their dips;
To wash away their karmas and pains,
It takes that water to remove those stains.

But up in the village of Goindwal,
In a sacred house with a peg in the wall,
Lived Guru Amar Das, the third Guru,
In the place where Arjan was born and grew.

I walked those streets to find that place
Where Guru sat in His sacred space,
Each step brought me closer to understand
That this path was carved by Guru's hand.

For against that wall Guru would sit
And Fate and Destiny He would knit
Together in His meditations deep;
With His hair tied up, so He wouldn't sleep.

Around that peg His hair was tied,
To wake Him up whenever He tried
To sleep, instead of meditate:
It pulled Him up to stay awake.

And I understood, when I saw that wall,
That this path is the same for us all;
That only when we sit and meditate
Can we find the substance that makes us great.

It is the same for me, the same for you
As it was the same for each Guru;
That day-by-day we must sit and grind
Ourselves slowly, slowly but exceedingly fine.

That wooden peg is smooth and worn
In the house where Arjan was born,
For Guru was a man, like you or me,
Who followed this path to Victory.

Four hundred years later, here in the West,
Each new day we rise and face the test
To identify ourselves and stand our ground,
In this land where broken hearts are found.

The course hasn't changed since Guru's time,
We all must bow low to be divine,
Japa and Tapa we must combine
To give the light to shunya's shine.

Guru has walked this way before,
As I walk it now to find his door,
And it gives me hope when I recall
That humble peg in Goindwal.

Espanola, New Mexico
5 September, 1994

115

WITH HONOR

Dressed in Bana, White and Blue,
Shoulder to shoulder, two by two
With faces shining, swords in hand
And kirpans ready they took their stand,
To protect the beloved son of the Guru.

With their own youthful bodies they stood
Before the challenge, the bad and good,
Prepared to die, his honor to keep,
They never flinched or missed a beat,
Prepared to attack if they should.

Through the pressing crowds they led the way
With perfect discipline into the fray,
They kept the circle and held on tight,
Not showing doubt or sign of fright,
They protected his life day to day.

They stood at his door, strong and straight,
Like fearless sentries at Guru's gate,
Through long hot days and each dark night,
They stood their duty and stood it right,
For it is truly their destiny to be great.

They did it with joy, they did it with grace,
They did it with humor, at their own pace,
Though they ate all they could and often were loud,
They made a big mess, but we all were proud
Of each shining soul and innocent face.

Have no fear for the Future, have Faith!
The Future is sound, our Dharma is safe,
For upon those young shoulders the Future shall rest,
Thousands shall come to them to be blest
And from them, thousands shall find Grace.

With their own bodies, in that crushing heat,
They protected the Dharma; Let the enemies retreat!
Guru stands with them, in each beating breast,
For it is in the face of challenge that we find our best,
And with reverence I would kiss all their feet.

Soon the time will come for me to step aside,
I will do so with joy, I will do so with pride,
I will give them my badge, give them my stars,
For they will carry the spirit near and far,
I saw in them the future, and with joy I cried.

This is what they learn in that far away land,
They learn how to walk, they learn how to stand,
They learn to face fear, bearing Guru's shield,
And with Victory's lance, they learn not to yield,
For they are invincible, when together they band.

They are the Khalsa, let all the people know,
Raj Karegha Khalsa is the spirit that they show,
With their joy for living, they are spreading Guru's Light,
And by their radiant humor they do it with delight,
Guru's Grace and Mercy shall follow wherever they go.

Espanola, New Mexico
17 October, 1995

JIWAN MUKHT

The Ancient Cradle of Civilization,
The birthplace of our Khalsa Nation,
There, in the East, Mother India rests,
While Time itself upon her nests
And history turns its page.

The land of the Gurus, where all life began,
She holds the secrets of God to Man,
In her sorrow and spiritual heart
Waiting, waiting for life to start
In this, another Age.

Our Spiritual Legacy summons the Test,
While our Destiny calls us to the West;
That Guru's prophecy shall be fulfilled,
That mankind's madness might be stilled
Here, where hearts are broken.

Her seed we carry in our heart and head
And, like the pollen of the trees, we spread
Across this Earth, blown by Guru's breath,
Drifting, drifting to land here in the West,
Where Truth shall be spoken.

Big like the trees and with shade for all
We will grow in time, strong and tall,
Touching the sky with roots deep in the ground
And swaying in the wind of the Ancient sound
That is Infinity's Song.

We, the Children of the Cusp have come
To give Aquarius an Earthly home,
But, to our Mother India we bow,
For she has given us the Know and How,
It is to her that we belong.

Espanola, New Mexico
30 May, 1994

118

SLEEP

For just a few brief moments
Let me close my eyes,
I'll just rest here, upright,
Ow! I bit my tongue when my chin fell.
I'm okay, better hold my head up, though;
I can hear the voices
Close, yet so far away,
Drifting into the fog of my brain.....
What did he say?
I should reply,
Wait! That doesn't make sense.

Another speech so I think
We are safe here,
If only my head would stop nodding,
What? Yeah, okay. Thanks, I'm awake,
Just meditating... and resting my... eyes....
Like vapor the consciousness is gone.......
Hey! Who hit me in the face?
They knocked my turban sideways!
These people can be so rude.
Uh, oh excuse me.
Wahe Guru ji!

Quick, get Shanti!

Between Albuquerque and Los Angeles
35,000 Feet
8 March, 1995

THE STAIN

I am home now and my belly gurgles and spews,
There is goo in my lungs and my bowels are loose,
The dirt under my nails is just beginning to fade
And there are indelible stains in the clothes I had made,
Which won't ever wash out and the smell won't go,
My sinuses drip green and perpetually flow,
I can't stay awake, neither can I sleep,
I forget where I am and occasionally I weep:
I've touched the dust of India, and that memory now I keep.

The stains in my clothes, as if dyed, will not fade,
The smell in my nostrils recalls the pilgrimage that I made,
Each step I take, though home, retraces those I walked there,
Upon that warm, white marble, through the thickness of the air,
Stepping around the bodies in calm and sweet repose,
(Although there were times when I had to hold my nose),
Yet in that silent space, resting still in the night,
We walked with reverent Grace, bowing low to reach the height,
While all around us, like on a midway, was flashing light.

The stains are still on my feet, still upon my soles,
The pollution hides in my lungs, escaping through my nose,
But the dye of the Divine has stained the fabric of my heart,
And I hold that experience tightly and from it I'll never part,
Long after my clothes are cleaned and again my lungs are clear,
The touch of forehead upon that marble is the one thing I'll hold
dear,
Even though I'm home and by this illusion I am bound,
That stain upon my heart is where my thoughts are found,
And in the dusty back streets of my mind I hear that haunting
sound.

Let this stain remain upon my heart, let all of me be dyed
With the color of the Guru, who is ever by my side,
He also walks in front of me, to lead me day to day,
While bringing up the rear, in case I lose my way,
Which has been known to happen, perhaps a time or two
But, there to get my attention has been that son of the Guru,
Who has showed me how to walk upon this dusty road,
And how to stand up straight while bearing a heavy load,
For upon that humble head, the spiritual crown was bestowed.

So, let this prayer be answered, that I never again become clean,
Rather, let this stain spread into my every seam,
For I walked upon that marble, guided again by Guru's beam
And I stepped into that water in the fulfillment of a dream,
And dipped down with my master, from whose wisdom I have gleaned,
That it is only upon the Guru that any wise man will lean,
To sustain him through the challenges that human life will bring.
Soon my nose will clear and my lungs will stop producing green,
But that stain will never leave me, at least that is how it seems.

Espanola, New Mexico
13 October, 1995

121

THE YATRA

For twenty hours we hung in the air
Then, gently, in Dehli we landed with care,
The officers looked tired as they stamped us through,
But looking down the line, I saw that we were, too.
Yet we were excited, charged and alive
As we waited at the carousel for our luggage to arrive.

At the Park Hotel we got checked in,
Our luggage came up, we changed, and then
Into the taxis, through the awakening streets
To the old part of Dehli, past the police in their jeeps;
To Sis Ganj Gurdwara, through the noise and the crowd,
Up the wet marble steps and before the Guru we bowed.

We stood for *Ardas* at the sound of the drum,
It seemed like home, after how far we had come,
Then after prasad we pushed our way to the cars,
And to Bangla Sahib, through Dehli we charged,
Across the sky was the first stroke of light,
Bringing the day by erasing the night.

We dashed back to the hotel for a quick cup of tea,
Now that I think of it, I believe I had three,
Then back to the taxis, there was someone to see,
We had someplace to go and somewhere to be.
The driver blew his horn as we rounded the hubs
While Shanti went back for the gift of the golf clubs.

For another week we moved at that pace,
To one place, then to the other we raced,
Our clothes and our bags were covered with dirt,
Most of the time we were so tired, it hurt,
Our lungs filled with smoke, our eyes burned from the dust,
Our tummies were gurgly, but we maintained our trust.

We found spiders in our beds and hair on our sheets,
Smells from the devil and people touching our feet,
We squatted in the shower and, of course, for number two,
Yet Guru, through His mercy, always saw us through,
We worked through our changes, we worked through the crowd,
We worked through our karma, we cried and laughed out loud.

It was more than a journey, it was more than a test,
At Akal Takht we were honored, at Harimander we were blessed,
At Jalundur we were abused, at Anandpur we were praised,
Yet across the Punjab, the banner of the Khalsa we raised,
And the time is coming soon when we'll cross the sky again
To touch those sacred places and count the days until it ends.

Espanola, New Mexico
10 July, 1995

SARDAR JI

Hey, Sardar ji, I saw you there,
Like a perfect Englishman you were dressed with care,
Your jacket was square, your tie was right
And around your chin, your beard was tied tight,
Yet, I don't understand why, to prove that you are great,
You try to imitate that which you so hate.

Oh, Sardar ji, many times I heard you speak,
With your beard plastered to your face, just like a freak,
And though each word you spoke was chosen with great care,
It confirmed beyond all question that you are unaware,
But you spoke very well, very loud and long,
While the sound of your own voice, carried you along.

Yet, Sardar ji, as you are such a great Sikh,
It must make no difference that, simply, you are weak
And corrupt and sick right through your soul
Because, to receive a saropa seems to be your only goal,
Yet, if you're so great, with your beard tied tight,
Then why do you need Johnny Walker, so you can sleep at
night?

Hey, Sardar ji, take a long look around.
Do you see your Dharma breaking and crumbling down?
Do you see your children drifting far away?
Do you have the capacity to inspire them all to stay?
Do you have the depth to make them understand?
Do you have the living experience of Guru's hand?

So, Sardar ji, simply pour another round,
Then accept another saropa, while you ignore the sound
Of thousands of scissors snipping and razors across the skin
Of all your sons and daughters who have lost the will to win,
Then make another speech and continue with your dream
Of that day, which will never come, when you're accepted by
the Queen.

Between Delhi and Frankfurt
33000 Feet
28 February, 1995

THE MASTER

THE WAKE UP CALL

"Wake up!" he said, like thunder from the Skies,
"Wake up, my son and open your eyes.
Open your eyes and face the light,
Look for the Truth, you have that right.
Wake up my boy, you must understand,
Your destiny is marked by Guru's Hand."

With a sleepy voice I asked, "But How?
I've been dreaming too long to wake up now,
This blanket is warm, my dreams are sweet
And your path feels cold under my feet.
Let me stay here, just let me rest,
Go and find another fool to test."

"Sorry my Love, but your time has come
To leave this hotel and find your way home,
You have no choice, there is no other way,
You have come to go, you're not here to stay.
There's a job to do and it will not wait,
Get up now, you're already late!"

I pulled the blankets over my head
And closed my eyes, pretending to be dead,
But he wasn't fooled, he continued to speak,
"Get up, you nut; you must be great, not weak,
Now stand up straight, face the light, be strong,
To waste yourself here is dumb and wrong."

"But," I said as I again turned away,
"There are no buts, get *your* butt out' a the way,
And on your two feet, arise and stand!
You are no longer a child, you must be a man."
"I must be a man? I don't know how!"
"I'll show you my son, so get up - *now!*"

I pulled myself up, my feet found the floor,
And true to his word, he showed me the door
To my destiny, the way to be a man,
"Kindly show it to others, whenever you can,"
Was what he told me before I stepped through,
As the door closed behind me, my gratitude grew.

For many years now, he has walked with me,
He has been my guide; he has been my lee,
He has stood with me, even when I was wrong,
His compassion has been vast, his patience, long,
He has never faltered, never failed to act,
He has never turned and never looked back.

My long night ended with his wake up call,
That long nightmare and the long dark fall,
And by his grace, I have landed on my feet,
To walk beside him, through bitter and sweet,
I became a man, he showed me how.
Now, with deepest gratitude, I humbly bow.

Espanola, New Mexico
30 October, 1995

WHILE YOU WERE AWAY

I missed you while you were away and I stayed here behind,
A punishment worse than death, a penance for the cursed,
   A torture of heart and soul.
I did the job day to day, though you were ever on my mind,
Our wounded child, who suffered so long, with care
   I lovingly nursed
And prayed that she be restored whole.

You did the job, day to day, despite your suffering and pain,
A few steps closer to the open door you marched with noble
grace, to muted arrhythmic cadence.
You carried, with calm stability, your wracked and shuttering
frame
And bowed your fevered forehead, golden light upon your face,
To the One who gave you patience.

It is that gift of patience that has allowed me to stay with you,
Which has forgiven (though not forgotten) and made me try
again to finally get it right.
It is that selfless compassion, despite the crazy things I do,
Which gives me hope, despite the errors, that still somehow,
I can win this never-ending fight.

I missed you while you were gone and I stayed here behind,
Though I could not ease your pain, I couldn't help you stand,
   Still, I did my duty.
Next time though, when it's time to go, perhaps you'll
   keep me in mind
Or, perhaps we'll have gotten it right by Guru's hand.
In that there will be great beauty!

Los Angeles, California
22 December, 1996

ON MY BIRTHDAY

Sometimes we try and do our best,
Sometimes, though we try, we fail the test,
Sometimes we feel we deserve more,
Sometimes we long for Guru's shore,
(But mostly we want more).

I look at you and fail to understand
The full impact of Guru's hand,
But you give me hope and push me along,
Whether what I do is right or wrong,
(Though, mostly it is wrong).

So on this day I started this life,
Without understanding its clash or strife,
Only your guidance has seen me through
And set me straight on what to do,
(Mostly, I don't know what to do).

Someday I'll be a great teacher like you,
Then I can tell others what to do,
Only then can I show my gratitude,
When I can adjust another's attitude,
(Usually they are wrong).

So please accept this simple gift
As partial payment for the lift
You have given my heart and life,
For seeing me through my joy and strife,
(Mostly, joy through strife).

Albuquerque, New Mexico
22 September, 1994

129

THE CALL OF DUTY

For the Call of Duty he rises each day,
Though his body cries out and begs to stay,
But Duty is his Sovereign, so he serves to obey,
Then, with bright eyes flashing he enters the fray.

The pain runs deep, yet he stands tall and proud,
He does not falter, nor cry aloud,
He has never retreated, never cowed,
For to his Sacred Self, his head is bowed.

However painful the job may be,
However difficult the choice he sees,
Whatever the Call of Duty may be,
He always delivers unto Victory.

His heart, though broken, continues to shine
With that shimmering radiance we call Divine,
Magnified by the shining steel of his spine,
Yet, he makes no claim and denies, "Not mine."

The Call of Duty is the song he sings,
The Way of Duty is the Path he brings,
Devotion to Duty is what it means
For those who call themselves Kaurs and Singhs.

The Call of Duty has brought him here
And the Call of Duty has made it clear
That *WE* must stand and dismiss our fear,
Then carry his mission, far and near.

Espanola, New Mexico
18 April, 1996

GOOFY

Once on a hot Sunday afternoon
When we sat together at the table,
There were smiles and laughter in the room
And you spoke, as only you are able,
To each of us, unbalanced or stable,
And you gave me your plate, your food and spoon.

You turned your gaze and talked about me
With your radiant smile, I felt a touch of Bliss,
You said I was fine, as far as you could see,
With one exception, which you called my goofiness,
Poetry and philosophy are fine, yet I am amiss,
When I break down, act weird and become goofy.

I have acted goofy, oh, perhaps a time or two,
And each time you have brought me back
From the abyss of the goofy things I do,
And you have kept me, despite how I act,
Despite my goofiness, despite my lack,
On the sacred path of the Guru.

Remember the time that I bent this way?
It was a little goofy, but so intense!
I thought about that the other day,
And from that perspective it made no sense.
Then my sense of gratitude became immense,
For you held me and did not turn away.

There was that other time that was kind of weird,
More dumb than goofy, I suppose,
I was twisted, my perceptions were smeared,
I was blocked like water in a knotted hose,
Thick like the mud at the roots of the rose,
Yet as you yelled, you smiled behind your beard.

You've had to yell, sometimes loud and long,
You've had to push and punch and pull,
I've stumbled and straightened, been weak and strong,
Charged straight ahead like a wounded bull,
Continued eating though my belly was full,
Yet, you never gave up, even though I was wrong.

Though I've been a little goofy through the years,
We've both held on tight, through thick and thin,
We've sweated and bled and shed our tears,
For each other, and the victory we shall win,
I don't know if we could endure it all again,
But your memory and touch of grace I hold dear.

Espanola, New Mexico
21 August, 1995

MY LONGING

I long to bow with you on that Sacred Land,
To bow with you before the Father we share,
Who keeps us safe by His love, ever in His care,
Who keeps us ever covered with His own hand.
Here, beneath the ticking of my heart, I find
The painful longing, longing of my mind,
Like a beached whale, dying of thirst in the sand.

It is the call of duty, an old soldier's prayer
When the saber is shattered and broken,
For the voice of the cannon has spoken
And the once green fields lay smoking and bare;
To stand in the line of fire, calm before the charge,
Unflinching before the guns, their muzzles looming large
And surrender to Guru's Will without a care.

Tell me in front of what wall I must stand
That your caliber can penetrate my heart,
Fire the round straight and true, blow my life apart!
That at least my Sacred Soul can touch that Land.
Then, this bitter nightmare will have ended,
My broken heart will be cured and mended,
My Master, please give me that last command.

I long to walk with you in that Sacred Space,
I long to feel that wet dirt between my toes,
I long to see when that golden reflection glows
In the still, cold water of our Guru's Grace,
I long to step with you in the dark of night
In that pure, cold water where the fishes bite,
And see that golden glow upon your sweet face.

Oh, beloved Guru of Miracles, please listen!
My Master doesn't hear my solemn prayer,
Though he knows this breaking heart longs to be there
And see upon the marble his wet feet glisten,
And bow with him at the place of our birth,
And pray before the Crown of planet Earth,
And see upon the marble his wet feet glisten.

Espanola, New Mexico
7 October, 1996

133

MAN OF HONOR, MAN OF GRACE

Great strength of character upon his face,
Serene and quiet in his sacred space,
Negativity vanishes without a trace,
As devotion appears to take its place.
Such is the calibre of this Man of Grace.

The path of Honor is the Path he walks,
Infinite Truth he speaks, when he talks,
For the shroud of Maya is the foe he stalks,
While the cracks of consciousness with Truth he caulks,
And from that sacred quest, he never balks.

With generous heart and humble mind
He lightens the load of each soul he finds,
Penetrating vision he bestows on the blind
And heart and head, with Guru's love he binds,
While each word he speaks is comforting and kind.

Guru's Grace is the gift he brings to us all,
To lift us up when we stumble and fall,
To give us hope when our backs are to the wall,
He gives without measure, has sacrificed all,
For he rises to each challenge, when given the call.

A Man of Honor is the demand of the Age,
For a Man of Grace shall write History's page,
He will walk with dignity through Maya's rage,
And the time is now, he is upon the stage,
That humble and honorable Aquarian sage.

Los Angeles, California
14 April, 1996

134

MY MASTER

At the root of myself, through the thick green slime,
Below the shining surface, beyond the grasp of Time;
There, the root runs deep, losing its identity with the mud,
Where the water increases density, changing into blood,
Before the spark of synapse can cross the gap of grey,
Before the opaque orbs can perceive the light of day,
Or the air, which was the beginning, can roll into the breath,
Then escape into the ethers defining life and death,
There you are in your ecstasy, the unchanging paradigm!

At that point where doubt condenses into fear,
Before the chime of mourning tolls loudly in my ear
And the tears of grief and sorrow roll streaming down my
face,
Before I cross that line between honor and disgrace,
Where many before have fallen and many more may slip,
Where many lives drift empty, like a plague upon a ship;
At that point where fear begins to roll into despair,
Yet fails to yield to desperation, as hope takes to the air,
There you are, My Beloved, to let the Truth appear!

Espanola, New Mexico
11 June, 1996

135

MASTER OF THE MOMENT

Each breath he draws is by his command,
Each heartbeat is by strength of his will,
He directs his pranas to firmly stand,
So the order of destiny can be filled,
Then he faces the call of duty at will.

Each situation is under his control,
Each circumstance is clearly defined,
This body mare is reined in by his soul
With a touch that is powerful, yet refined,
Fully contained by the vastness of his mind.

He calls upon resources we can't see
Because our vision is blocked by doubt,
But the depth of his focus has set him free,
And like rain, he moves across the Earth to scout
For those fallen seeds that are ready to sprout.

Across the electric hum of the telephone lines,
After we have been tranquilized by sleep and dreams,
He extends his touch beyond the boundaries of Time,
Beyond the capacity of ordinary means;
To make us understand, all is not as it seems.

Ever unabashed and never afraid,
Never threatened, confused or lost,
Victory is the grit from which he is made
And he achieves it, no matter the cost,
Polishing each old soul to its brightest gloss.

He is never without words or a meaningful glance,
He says it all with an expression or a wink,
He directs the energy, leaving nothing to Chance,
Causing everyone to inhale and think,
Rewriting destinies with indelible ink.

He is Master of the Moment, Master of the Day,
Master of the Heart and Mind,
He walks with dignity on Guru's way,
Bringing hope to every soul he finds,
And with that touch, none shall be left behind.

Los Angeles, California
9 May, 1996

136

OBEDIENCE

Is it sufficient on my part,
When my head overrules my heart,
And all my anger, doubt and fear
Make you seem more far than near;
Is it then enough to obey?

When you speak and still I doubt,
Or answer with silence, to freak me out
And my mind, depressed, breaks apart,
While frustration and fear eat my heart;
Is it then enough to obey?

When I'm spinning 'round and 'round,
Feet to the sky, head to the ground,
When my Faith and Trust have disappeared,
Yet you smile at me, behind your beard,
Is it then enough to obey?

Is it sufficient, when in my heart,
I see my hope and joy depart,
Yet life goes on and I begin
To spin myself around again;
Is it then enough to obey?

When I question, instead of love,
When it's my anger I'm thinking of,
When I want to fight and disagree,
When I lose my vision and cannot see,
Is it then enough to obey?

How can I love you, when doubt is so strong,
Why do I question, when I know I am wrong?
How can I excel and find my way,
If I cannot serve you, then obey,
Isn't *to obey* the last step to Love?

For to love you, I must serve you,
No matter what my mind puts me through,
And when I serve in an acceptable way,
You give me, then, the chance to obey,
Isn't *to obey* the last step to Love?

Serve to obey, that's the way we start,
Then *obey to love*, to open the heart,
Love to excel and pass the test,
Then *excel to infinity*, to cover the rest,
Isn't *to obey* the last step to Love?

If I can obey and cross that line
Where my love is true and ever shines,
If I can love and then excel
And shine on brightly, through the Hell,
Then it will be enough to obey.

Rome - December, 1990
Revised - Espanola, 5 December, 1994

TO MY MASTER

This life I lay at your feet,
This soul I trust to your care,
The challenge to grow I will meet
And what I learn, I will share.

That which was distant is now at hand,
That which was prayed for now has come,
Before the fools I'll take a stand
And show the splendor of the One!

And from this day the past is dead,
I forgive myself the wrongs I've done,
Beneath the steel I've placed my head,
Oh! My master lead me home!

The time has come for me to rise,
Aweigh the anchor of the past,
To bear the weight of the times
Upon the depths of consciousness.

So when you hear that loving call
And Guru takes you in His arms,
I vow, the banner shall not fall,
But stand unfurled, safe from harm.

Santa Fe, New Mexico
Baisakhi, 1989

TO OUR MASTER

Our Lives, We lay at your feet.
Our Souls, We trust to your care.
The challenges to grow, We rise and meet,
And what We learn, that We share.

That which was distant is now at hand,
That which was prayed for now has come,
Before the fools We'll take a Stand
And Prove the Splendor of the One!

And from this day the past is dead!
We forgive each other the wrongs We've done,
Beneath the steel, We've placed our heads,
That Guru, through you, can lead us home!

The time has come for Us to rise,
Aweigh the anchor of the past;
To bear the weight of the times
Upon the depths of consciousness.

For upon those waters you've laid the keel,
Our songs are the wind that sets the bow,
We hold the rudder, forged of steel
And through the storm this ship will plough!

So when you hear that loving call
And Guru takes you in His arms,
We vow, the banner shall not fall,
But stand, unfurled, safe from harm!

Espanola, New Mexico
3 January, 1995

THE WEIGHT

It must have been painful in those tragic days
When he said you would never see him again,
When he told you, "You are the Master now."
That weight fell upon you in various ways,
Taking your youth and all that before had been,
Molding you into what you have become now.

Was the achievement of such a great thing,
An accomplishment longed for by most,
Less sweet with that bitter dose; while Life
As you had known it before you was unraveling?
Did you feel like a rudderless ship drifting along the coast?
Did that separation cut deep like a newly sharpened knife?

Did it feel any different to be the Master,
Different than being the student
Of such an extraordinary man?
Was he an extraordinary man like you, my Master;
To have pushed you up such a great ascent
And was, perhaps, no more a man than you are a man?

Did you believe him when he said that to you?
If you told me that today, could I carry on?
Perhaps it's the fear of that which holds me back.
If you told me that today, would I believe you?
Would I pick up the banner and carry on
Before it touched the ground and fell slack?

Perhaps it's the fear of that which holds me back,
Perhaps it's the fear of bearing that unbearable weight,
Yet, if we walk this path with you, then we *must* bear that load.
It has to fall on each of us, despite our doubt or lack,
For it's in the act of bearing it that makes one great
And, in reality, I think it doesn't fall but is bestowed.

Los Angeles, California
2 May, 1997

141

THE TOUCH OF THE MASTER

*On the Occasion of the 66th Birthday
of the Siri Singh Sahib*

The touch of the master is what brought us here,
Through Maya's illusion, through doubt and fear,
We have followed him through this long, dark night,
To awaken from the dream, and face the light.
Now the time has come, we must rise and stand,
And reverently take the reins from his steady hand,
This is the birthday gift that would mean the most.

From thousands of wounds sustained along the way,
He is covered with scabs, yet he faces the fray
With smiles and laughter and a thundering voice,
Driving us to the point where we have no choice
Except to stand strong, with courage and win the fight,
For there is no substitute for victory, no greater delight,
Victory is the birthday cheer he would like to toast.

Deep in his breast his patched up heart beats on,
Broken by the past but sustained by the song
Of his longing and a deep love for his Guru,
Which he has brought to us here, for me and you.
We have heard that song, let us sing together now,
Let our voices rise and in gratitude let us bow.
Let Gratitude be the birthday candle that we light.

His beard has turned white, yet still he stands straight,
Unbroken by Time, he has shouldered its weight.
He was attacked from the front and from the rear,
He was attacked over there and over here,
He has defended our Dharma and upheld her grace,
And defeated her enemies, who fell in disgrace.
Now, on this birthday, let *us* take the fight.

Steady as stone and unbending as steel,
Mind like a computer and heart like a wheel,
Compassion is the law that governs his life.
No matter the conflict, no matter the strife,
He has never given up, nor let us down,
And he is ready, again, to walk another round,
For this birthday, let *us* carry the weight,

The touch of the master has brought us so far
He has illumined our path, like a shining star,
With dignity, he bears the torch of Guru's light
And with patience, he pushes us to get it right.
The touch of the master, gift of the Divine,
Has polished our steel, now brightly, let us shine,
For this birthday let us prove that we are great!

Espanola, New Mexico
26 August, 1995

TO TELL THE TRUTH

You called me late one January night
When fatigue had sucked the life from my blood,
I lay in the darkness, more dead than asleep,
While drifts of dream began to occlude
The fragile connection with Earth that I keep,
Then the telephone startled me with fright.

Your familiar voice was warm through the wires
And from my solitary void drew me out,
I felt cold as we spoke, sitting in the dark
Then, when the moment came, you didn't shout
But, though you asked softly, it found its mark
And my heart seized, as though pinched by pliers.

In each life comes a critical moment
When we face that transitional point in Time,
The chance to transcend instinct and reason
And that particular moment was mine,
On that silent night in the cold, dark season,
And the Truth bound me to you like cement.

I told the Truth when you asked me that question,
Though like lightening a lie crossed my mind,
But Guru's Grace gave me the strength to speak
And though painful, no regrets do I find,
Though afterward, in the dark, I felt weak
From that solitary moment of confrontation.

I do not claim to be a hero today,
Yet by the Code of the Warrior that night,
I did what was honorable for Duty,
What I did, though simple, was right.
And in that action I found great beauty,
This is the dignity of Guru's way.

I will be grateful for all of my days
That you gave me that most difficult test;
The chance to face the challenge of Time,
Then bring out of my noble Self the best,
And save my Sacred Honor from the grime.
I will be grateful all of my days.

Los Angeles, California
June, 1996

PERSPECTIVES
OF A PILGRIM

THE FIVE KRIYAS*

"Guru Ram Das Kriya," the first I learned,
Came as a gift, it was unearned,
Three hours a night the energy tripped
Throat, to heart, to navel, to lips.

This kriya removed my illusion and strife,
And I pray that I do it the rest of my life,
It gave me the living vision of the Guru
And if you practice, you will have that too.

Then came "Sushumna," gift of Guru,
I was in the gurdwara when I knew
The sweet secret of the twenty-six strokes,
Which transforms even us hopeless folks.

Throat, to heart, to navel, to crown
While repeating the sacred sound;
Crown to ajna, but in two parts,
Then again the divine cycle starts.

"Sidh Karm Kriya," which we call *Tershul*,
Can be practiced and perfected by any fool;
Place your hands in the Trident then you
Repeat *Har Har Wahe Guru.*

From the fingers the lightening goes
And from the navel the energy flows,
The three gunas come under your command,
Then a healing touch comes in your hands.

Then "So Darshan Chakra Kriya" I learned,
It didn't come easy, the results hard earned,
In through the ida, the prana flows,
And out through the pingla, apana goes.

Recite *Wahe Guru* before you release
And pump the navel to find your peace,
Sixteen times multiplied by four throws,
With eyes affixed at the tip of the nose.

Then "Nabhi Kriya" with Trikurti came,
In Shuni Mudra you recite the Name
By pumping the navel out and in,
With the eyes focused at the chin.

Let the breath flow and this you do:
Recite *Har Hare Hari Wahe Guru.*
When you practice, comes knowledge of all things,
Depth and intuitive understanding it brings.

All channels flow into these five
And you must do them to survive
This time of the Cusp, which will test
Each of us who fail to do our best.

But hear this warning above all,
The higher you go, the further you fall
And if you fail to practice with gratitude,
You will lose your space and latitude.

Frustration will come to torture you,
So appreciate these gifts of the Guru,
It is the subtle experience that you gain
When you practice and recite the Name.

Look deep, and listen, and reflect
If these kriyas you are to perfect,
They do not come as a flash of light
But softly, as a breeze in the night.

And as with a narcotic, you will be hooked,
For by your experience you will be shook,
So practice with reverence and do your best,
And if you keep up, you will be blest.

I request this prayer of the True Guru,
To be granted to anyone who
Reads these words and these kriyas tries,
That they attain the perfection of their lives.

Espanola, New Mexico
14 May, 1994

See the Appendix for a description of each Kriya.

AKAL

With Deathless courage we started our quest!
With naïve innocence we pushed from the heart
And by the Code of the Warrior we did our best,
For it was that spirit which gave us our start;
So long ago, when we were still young at heart.

The White Hawk rises, surrounded by blue,
Such strength of spirit and serenity of soul,
Which comes from that deathlessness, known only by few
Who have touched that Sacred Space that makes us whole,
And the quest for that consciousness has been our goal.

The Primal Power is the shield he proudly bears
Where at the Point of Truth the balance is hung.
It cuts both ways, is the understanding that he shares,
Whether the power of the sword or that of the tongue,
For Truth shall prevail wherever it is rung.

And that totality, like the sacredness of the womb,
When touched by the Soul and blessed through Grace,
Is safely protected. There righteousness shall bloom,
And with those two blades God defends that space,
For, He holds us between them in His Deathless embrace.

In God We Trust reads the banner between the wings,
Flying proudly above all, defending the shield,
For trust in God is what our Deathlessness brings,
It is the One power to which we yield
And is the double-edged sword that we wield.

May that Deathless courage never leave us,
That we may always follow our quest for the heart,
May the Code of the Warrior ever inspire us
And let us remember the innocence of our start,
That our victorious spirit may never depart.

Los Angeles, California
10 March, 1997

BEFORE YOU GO

Just one last thought before you go,
A final word before you leave,
On this loom, the tapestry shall grow
In the excellence which you weave;
Excellence, which we vow to show.

Trust everyone for nothing today,
But trust that Guru will come through,
That Sacred Trust we shall not betray,
Our colors, though faded, stand true,
For Guru's order we serve to obey.

Though we are funky we've shown grit,
Though we are lazy and tend to whine,
Though we are stained, we're hard as the pit,
And if even once you've seen us shine
Let that confirm that the torch has been lit.

Though we wait until forced to act,
A bad habit we haven't outgrown,
Together we have forged this pact
That, together our destiny is sewn,
And that seam shall remain intact.

The Children of the Cusp are we,
Two steps forward and one back we go,
But we'll all get there, just wait and see,
Though our pace might seem a bit slow,
With a touch of Chanel and Armani.

We will do it with humor and with grace,
We will do it with joy and with style,
We will carry that torch at a regal pace
And we'll stop for pizza once in a while,
For slow and steady will win the race.

As Siblings of Destiny we stand,
Before our Guru we kneel and bow,
As soldiers we obey your command
And before Mukunday we make this vow,
That to all we will extend our hand.

Just one last thought before you go,
That together, forever we are bound,
Unto Mankind that Grace shall flow,
For wherever a longing is found
Shall never be heard the word "No."

Espanola, New Mexico
8 October, 1996

THE SLEEPING YOGINI

In eternal sleep, across the land she lies,
Silent and still as the dark of night,
Beneath the Heavens and the Infinite Skies,
Beneath the Moon and stars of light,
Over her shadow the White Hawk flies.

Her sacred form only a few will know,
Her secret silence only a few will hear,
By light of the Moon she will only glow,
For the Sun must enter in to make clear
The secrets she will not show.

By day she is a shadow, long and still,
By night she is hidden from the blind,
But from that point below La Bajada Hill,
If her sleeping, silent form you can find,
Then her secret wisdom she might spill.

The White Hawk soars in his silent flight,
Ever deeper, deeper into the Blue
And the Sleeping Yogini, still as the night,
Holds the secrets she will give only to you,
Find her and hold her wisdom tight.

Below the surface of that ancient sea,
You'll find her sleeping upon its floor,
From the house of the Moon, by the Sun you'll see,
Understand her silence to find the door
And know her secret to find the key.

Espanola, New Mexico
19 May, 1995

BETWEEN ALBUQUERQUE
AND SANTA FE

The sun pitched down beneath the sheltering blue,
Though the highway seemed out of place upon the land,
While in a wheezing old car I accelerated through
My misery and anger against that Mighty Hand.

The car sucked wind with shuddering fibrillation
As I pushed it over the hills and up the road;
Climbing over the recesses of argument and imagination,
Looking for a proper destination to drop my load.

These fleeting circumstances through Time and Space
Formed kind of a roadblock along the Infinite Way,
Throwing me off my course and altering the pace,
Obscuring the light of that incredible day.

The Sleeping Yogini, in her silence so still,
Lay behind me while my thoughts drilled in deep,
As I looked in the mirror from La Bajada Hill,
I longed to tap that patience which she keeps.

I rolled down into Santa Fe, lost in a dream,
Locked in combat with the demons of my mind,
We fought in silence, I couldn't shout or scream
And on the radio, nothing good could I find.

Then a thought leaked into the cacophonous sound
That raged on deafeningly in a place so small,
For, contained within a glob of only three pounds
Were the argument and the solution to it all.

I remembered, though miraculously it seemed,
The advice of Guru Nanak to idiots such as me,
"If you don't like it, complain to God," he beamed,
"Because the lock is only opened with His key."

So I spoke to God as I would speak to a friend,
Well, perhaps a friend who had wrecked my car,
I told Him I thought that this situation should end
That, as God, he could do much better, by far.

I don't mean to imply that my speech was rude,
Only expressive in a more creative way,
Though my language was colorful, it wasn't crude
And He listened to everything I had to say.

The thing about God that I have found
Is He listens and seldom interrupts,
Like the Sleeping Yogini, He utters no sound,
Regardless of what discussion erupts.

I had erupted enough and settled down,
As the car rattled and hummed along the street,
Through the streets of Santa Fe I silently wound
Then I stopped to get something to eat.

I thought to myself, some sign would be cool,
Some indication that I had been noticed and heard,
Something to pull me out of the spinning whirlpool,
To make me feel balanced and a little less absurd.

I looked ahead through the windshield, not very far
And laughed aloud as I stared through the glass,
For a faded bumper sticker on a beat up old car
Read, in large purple letters, *"THIS TOO SHALL PASS."*

Though God is a Loner, His sense of humor is great,
And a few words of thanks I whispered with a smile,
Then I prayed that Guru Nanak, who set me straight,
Will still be with me after I've crossed my last mile.

Los Angeles, California
5 June, 1996

THE CITY OF THE ANGELS

The City of the Angels surrounds me,
Deafening noise rises up from the street,
The smog impairs my ability to see,
Smothering the Earth with its own heat,
Adding a labor to every heartbeat.

The evening sky is churned by the rotors,
While those with desperate heart run to hide,
On the street the police rev their motors,
Pursued by their desperation inside,
Riding over the remains of their pride.

Up in the hills a lost, broken dreamer
Turns from her shattered honor once more,
While her life flashes by like a streamer,
And not understanding what life was meant for,
She drifts further from sanity's shore.

On the streets crawl the lost and the broken,
Pushing the remnants of their lives in carts,
Mumbling words that will never be spoken;
They escaped through the cracks of broken hearts,
Instantly impaled by insanity's darts.

Through the smog the prayers of the Angels
Never stop and continue as before,
Perhaps lost at night by a siren's wail
Then, just before dawn, they are heard once more,
For below the rotors is Guru's door.

Every morning before the sea retreats,
Rolling back into itself for the day,
Before oil glistens on the City's streets,
Before traffic's fat has clotted the way,
Earthly angels pass through those doors to pray.

At those doors, through the darkness of the night,
While the rotors churn loudly in the sky,
Shines the Ruby of Guru's loving light,
As the wailing sirens go racing by,
It shines on brightly with sleepless eye.

The Prayers of the Angels surround me
Through the noises that rise up from the street,
Guru's Light enhances my ability to see,
Igniting the flame of the Kundalini's heat,
Bringing grace and joy to every heart beat.

Los Angeles, California
3 April, 1996

REFLECTIONS AT 40,000 FEET

In this silver tube I am crossing the sky
And I feel you tickling my soft heart,
Perhaps it is the clouds or depth of blue,
Perhaps at this altitude I feel closer to you,
Perhaps the possibility of death makes me start,
But, for some reason, I feel that I could cry.

My mind drifts, like the clouds below,
Thoughts pass like the green earth I see,
The silver clouds thicken, the sky grows dark
As I ponder, thickly, the flash of your arc
Across the dark gap of my uncertainty,
While the turbulence flicks us high and low.

Like this silver tube, through life we go,
Shaking and trembling against the storm,
We try to rise against the roiling air,
To change our course from here to there,
To rise above the threatening form
So that life's dark clouds drift far below.

I worry, I doubt, I'm still unsure
And, though I feel ashamed, I still argue
In my mind, like an old dog at night
Barking at the sky or a distant light.
Yet, like a fool, I still argue with you,
For no other reason than I am insecure.

Yet, in this silver tube I sit in this seat,
Rocking across the sky on unsteady air,
I trust the pilot who I cannot see,
I trust the engines screaming behind me,
I trust this silver tube will get me there
And that trust alone is an amazing feat.

Are you any less than that pilot up there?
Can't you navigate across this sky,
Supported by the wind and rising air,
Bound to your word by the strength of a prayer?
Across this universe is where you fly,
Though ever in motion, you are always here.

Like the scream of the engines to the clouds,
I hear the song of my heart and longing,
Like the flash of the lightening in my mind,
The call of your Name is what I find
That brings me nearer to my belonging
And like a shawl over my mind, your comfort shrouds.

Eventually, we'll land then I'll be free
Of this silver tube that has crossed the sky,
The cabin service will have come to an end
And we will all be invited to come again,
If we have another opportunity to fly,
And at the door, Your face I'll finally see.

Between Washington, D.C. and Albuquerque
40,000 feet
15 August, 1995

INSANITY

I'm insane! This I know to be true,
I should be dragged, then beaten with a shoe,
My eyes should be gouged; my ears should be cut,
My teeth should be pulled and my mouth sewed shut.
My hair should be plucked out, my skin should be stripped,
My nose should be stopped and my clothes should be ripped!

Take me by the fingers and drive slivers through the quick,
Hang me by my ankles and beat me with a stick,
Break my every bone, then turn me over the fire,
Tattoo across my forehead, *"Here's an Idiot and a Liar!"*
Throw me on the ground and like a dog, make me bark,
Then, please flip me over and stuff chilies where it's dark!

If I live in my depression and forget I have a Guru,
Or meditate for hours, then walk around feeling blue;
Then lock me in a closet and nail me to the floor,
Then release the snakes, and remember to lock the door.
If I don't feel grateful for every breath I take,
Then I am worse than stupid, I'm dishonest and a fake.

How can I love my madness more than I love the Truth?
I wander around in sadness like a melancholy youth,
I know what is the Reality, yet I'm trapped in Maya's dream,
And that is true insanity, for things are never as they seem.
Yet, I prefer to suffer, because that habit in me is strong,
I behave just like a duffer, even though I know it's wrong.

If I fail to excel, then I haven't done my best,
No point to scream and yell and blame it on the rest.
The problem lies with me, to find my grit and steel,
To eradicate my sorrow and bow to Guru's Will.
If I live this Dharma, how can I be sad and blue?
To continue with this drama is a direct insult to you.

I meditate in the morning, I meditate at night,
If I walk around in mourning, then something can't be right.
Then, I must be truly insane and sick right to my core!
So, when you see me coming, run and lock your door!
For, if you ever see me and I fail to show a smile,
Then tie me to your bumper and drag me for a mile.

One other possibility that I would like to share with you,
Why don't we join together and help each other through?
Why don't we make a contract to live with Joy and Grace
And celebrate by living with our gratitude in place?
Take it from a madman, who has suffered through every test,
We were not *meant* to suffer, but it takes Gratitude to find the
rest.

Espanola, New Mexico
14 December, 1994

IN MEMORY'S PASSION

I miss you now, after all these years,
After Time's caress has dried the tears,
After Duty has been paid its due.
There are moments, more than a few,
When my mind reaches out to find you,
Calling to the heart, "What have we done?"
Now, only the memory lingers.
The answer doesn't come, there isn't one.

Like India ink upon a white sheet
You have dyed the fibers of my mind,
There are no regrets in each heartbeat,
Only tenderness is what I find.
And, when I assess what dear price I paid,
I will cherish, forever, that choice I made.

Espanola, New Mexico
26 March, 1996

NAV JIWAN KAUR

Softly she came, with deep blue eyes,
Late that night before Thanksgiving,
She never cried, just gasped, then sighed,
As she began the process of living
Her brief little life full of giving;
The Princess of the New Life.

Deep in her eyes, the Blue Ethers shined
As she lay quietly, swaddled and still,
So tiny she was, by God's design,
That only my hand could she fill,
Yet all of my heart did she thrill,
The Princess of the New Life.

It was the Year of the Comet,
That year when she was born,
And it rattled our minds like a jet.
Yet by her Peace, soft and warm,
My icy heart was transformed
By the Princess of the New Life.

She loved all the people around her,
She brought comfort and joy to their lives,
She sat in every lap that could hold her,
Bringing them joy and surprise
With the mischief in her eyes;
The Princess of the New Life.

One eye looked straight to the future,
One eye looked away and around,
For we were confused by our culture
And to our neuroses we were bound
And a balance she never found,
The Princess of the New Life.

Then one bright sunny morning
Under the deep blue sky,
Guru hugged her without warning,
She left her body, but didn't die,
For in my heart she's alive,
The Princess of the New Life.

Sometimes great souls come as children,
That God may touch us with His Grace.
And this little girl, so golden,
Brought His smile to every face,
Dressed in satin and lace;
The Princess of the New Life.

Espanola, New Mexico
21 November, 1994

MY PASSION

Are You
There at the end of my prayer,
When my mind cannot focus
And thoughts and questions
Crawl into the sacred space
Slowly?

Can You
Come to me in the dark of dawn,
Before the day rises against the
Flash and fusion of life ongoing
Day to day, while we spin
Silently?

Do You
Hear the ticking of my heart,
As it dutifully pumps the blood
Through emotions and commotions,
Not understanding that you have filled it
Sweetly?

Do You
Hear the song of my longing,
When the cars race past smoking
Or the telephone hums in my ear,
While my mind flies forward
Blindly?

Will You
Come to me now, quietly in the night,
Like the breeze in the summertime
After the sun has set and the heat
Rises in waves to the evening sky
Softly?

Espanola, New Mexico
15 June, 1994

IN THE AGE OF PISCES

All that we believe we shall defend,
Before *our* God the Infidel shall bend,
For the sinner's dereliction here must end.
We'll take their heads and hang them high,
Upon the rack we'll make them cry,
To redeem themselves before they die.
If they fail to confess or cry aloud,
If they stand bloody, yet unbowed,
If the demon in them waxes proud,
Then we'll set the flames and watch them burn,
For these are the wages that they've earned,
Though History's lesson we've never learned.
In the Name of God more people have died
At the hands of those, who through their pride,
Believed such atrocities were justified.
And slowly, our spirits were broken.

We closed our mouths afraid to speak,
We closed our eyes, afraid to peek,
We closed our minds so they wouldn't leak.
We bowed to the King to keep our heads
When they took our wives from our beds.
We accepted as truth whatever they said;
That they came from God and were divine,
That they were descended from a noble line,
That all was theirs and nothing was mine.
They took the lands wherever they could,
They started crusades and called them good
And all who opposed them tasted blood.
Yet they bowed to the Cross, the Crescent and Star;
In the name of religion they declared war,
From land to land and shore to shore
The peace was continually broken.

Heart after heart has been broken,
Drop after drop of blood has fallen,
Word after word has been spoken.
In the Name of God we drew the Sword,
For God and Country we gave our Word,
We stood in the stirrups as the line moved forward.
Our virgin blades flashed in the sunlight,
Our excited faces were shiny and bright,
Then we charged the enemy with all our might!
Smoke and leather, steel and lead,
Screams and blood, wet and red,
Our frightened faces sickened by the dead,
Our bloodied steel nicked and turned.
Throughout the Ages these fires have burned,
Yet History's lesson we've never learned.
And again, our hearts were broken.

So, in 1469 there came
A humble man who loved the Name,
Who taught others to do the same.
And so was turned history's page
By that simple and tireless sage,
Who is the Guru of the Aquarian Age.
There is no secret between God and Man,
If you recite the Name, then anyone can
Open his mind to understand
That God's not out there but here, within,
And all is written by His flowing pen,
Then Man's tyranny of the Mind must end.
Dharma is the path we walk
And Truth we speak, when we talk,
For Grace is bestowed, never bought.
And our hearts and minds have opened.

Espanola, New Mexico
3 July,1995

THE WHEEL

There is a scratch upon my stone, with grooves across the face,
Which run down to the edge then disappear without a trace,
They will not wash away; I can't hide them from my view,
They remain engraved upon my stone no matter what I do.
There is only one way to remove them, for my shining stone to heal:
My innocent stone must be polished by the Master Jeweler's wheel.

The wheel is spinning fast, the coarse surface blurred and wet,
The Master Jeweler takes my stone and to the wheel it's set,
Upon that tarnished surface the wheel begins to grind,
Turning stone to powder, leaving the past behind.
This simple act of love from a Jeweler to a stone,
Occurs without a word, a complaint or a groan.

Too often when my Master has held me to the wheel
To polish my blemished surface, I kick and loudly squeal,
"I do not need this now, let me live with this small blight,"
But with the patience of the Jeweler, he simply holds me tight,
"I will never let you go until the cut is right,
Until your shining radiance is that of Guru's Light."

Once again my stone is shining, once again it's clear,
Once again the Light refracts brightly through its sphere,
Just a little kiss to the face from that grinding wheel
Has made this rock more precious, made its value more real,
Made the deeply grooved surface smooth as it was before.
And placed into the setting, it lights me up once more.

I should learn a lesson from that humble stone of mine
And quietly face the wheel, instead of complain and whine,
Whenever the Master Jeweler touches the wheel to grind
Away those blemishes and grooves that run across my mind.
It is that selfless act of love that will cause my Soul to shine,
For in my Master's touch is the artistry of the Divine.

Espanola, New Mexico
23 January, 1997

THE POTTER

We are like those special jars that line the temple halls,
Which hold the fragrant oils or the butter and the milk,
We are found in those recesses of the sacred temple walls,
Resting in the cool darkness, wrapped up carefully with silk,
Illumined by a candle or a lamp.

We were formed upon the wheel at the Master Potter's feet,
His long, strong fingers probing our density and mass,
He spun us long and slow, while each cubic inch He beat,
To soften us as each dizzying turn made its pass,
While His moistened hands kept us soft and damp.

Once we were soft and smooth He accelerated the wheel
And began to lovingly shape this, our sacred form.
He worked with the soft clay, by projection and by feel,
And with water and friction, He kept us moist and warm,
Shaping us to the unchained melody of His will.

With a kick He spun us faster and began to slap the clay
And while spinning He formed us with His strong hand,
Yet He kept one hand inside so the softened shape would stay,
That unassisted, His graceful, shining form would stand,
So our precious contents could not spill.

He dried us in the Sun as we absorbed the blazing light,
Then He carefully glazed us, so we could not spring a leak
And He placed us in the fire, the jumping flames hot and bright,
And though He laughed and sang to us, seldom did He speak,
For the communication was that simple act itself.

He took us from the fire and gently cooled us in His stream,
Then carefully checked for the tiniest crack or phase
And those who remained smooth, who showed no crack or seam,
Who held together through that intense fire of the glaze,
Were ready to be filled and placed upon the shelf.

With His sacred essences He filled each gleaming jar,
Then proudly stamped each silken wrap with His seal
And some He has kept near to Him, some He shipped afar,
But each one is beloved and precious to Him, I feel,
For each one has been marked by His hand.

We are like those special jars, which line the temple halls
And we each hold that sweet element of His art,
We were formed to serve and contained within our walls
Is that sacred matter, which enriches the soul and heart,
And is the Grace by which we stand.

Los Angeles, California
20 Feb, 1997

THE PRISONER

The walls rise high all around me
And no exit or escape can I find,
There is no light or window to see,
For I'm a prisoner of my own mind
And in solitary I am confined.

Before the judge, in chains I stood.
When I looked, I saw that it was me,
Who sat in judgment, yet saw no good,
Who determined that I could not go free,
That a prisoner I would be.

"Remain in here, you little man,
There's no way out that you can see,
Try to find the door if you can,
And remember that you hold the key,
And only *you* can set yourself free."

I have lived in darkness all these years
And in solitude I have remained,
I have screamed aloud and shed my tears
Yet, still to these walls I am chained
And my freedom I have never gained.

Deep in the darkness, between these walls
The monsters come in to torture me,
No one responds to my screams and calls
For these demons only I can see
And only *I* can make them flee.

Understanding that, came a glint of light,
And under the mud stirred a prayer,
Then the glow of hope that yet, I might
Have the courage to walk out of there,
And delight in God's shining air.

Late that night when the demons came,
They came not from without, but within,
I faced them with joy and beat their game
And they have never come again,
Because they know they cannot win.

When the morning came the Sun shined in
And the towering walls I could not find,
Then I vowed to myself that never again
Would I be a prisoner of my own mind,
And I have left all my fears behind.

Espanola, New Mexico
21 May, 1995

STUPID

For so many years I have lived a lie,
For so many years I was wrong,
For so many years my heart would cry,
"I have no value, I don't belong,"
And for all those years I was wrong.

I believed I was not good enough
To be counted among the great,
I believed that I lacked the right stuff,
That inadequacy was my fate,
And that belief in me was great.

The insults I bore for all those years
Were like a gunshot wound to the head,
Self inflicted by my doubts and fears
And though breathing, my spirit was dead,
Killed by the delusion in my head.

I heaped such insults upon the One
Who created my heart and soul,
Who gave me breath, who wound and spun
That precious coil which makes me whole,
Which is the instrument of the soul.

My Master pushed even though I pulled,
He hammered until I was nailed,
He snorted and stomped, butted and bulled,
Until my shy excellence he had hailed
And Guru's seal upon me was nailed.

I understand now how stupid I've been
To have believed myself not enough,
That is, perhaps, the only True Sin
And it has only made my life more rough
And, believe me, it has been rough enough.

Los Angeles, California
9 January, 1997

THE CIRCLE

I sat upon the mountain and watched the waters rise,
As I called out to the Heavens above the clouded skies,
I watched the falling rains give momentum to the flood,
Which washed away the cultures and changed the Age for good.
When I stepped down from that mountain to the barren plain
below,
My Immortal God, across the sky, shined His bright rainbow.

I stood in the stone circle in those ancient days
And kept the secret teachings, followed the ancient ways,
I bowed to the sun at its zenith in the month of June,
And upon that wet, green grass I danced beneath the moon.
I lighted the fires at midnight and uttered the secret sounds,
Then walked with frightened reverence upon those sacred grounds.

I sat high up in the mountains, surrounded by the snow,
My mind suspended in the ethers, my breathing long and slow,
I never moved a muscle; I never uttered a sound,
Yet I probed those sacred spaces where the deities are found,
And wrestled with the demons in their misty dark domains,
Then sang the sacred hymns with their hauntingly sweet refrains.

The mystery of the galaxies I studied long and deep
And how to calculate a course across the desert's sweep,
I learned the incantations, which change matter into mass
And how to shatter light with a prismed piece of glass,
The properties of the essences like frankincense and myrrh,
I carried to that baby which caused the legend to occur.

I practiced those secret teachings with others in my home,
Then hid out in the caves around the Seven Hills of Rome,
I faced the red centurions when they took me with their spears,
Then stood on that bloodstained sand and quietly faced my fears.
I fought the gladiators and wrapped them in my net,
Then danced naked with the lions, their breath hot and wet.

I swung my heavy sword as I charged across the mud
And in the Name of God I spilled another's blood!
I stood tall in the saddle as I watched the advancing wraith,
Then firmly gripped my lance as I charged forth to defend the
Faith!
I engaged the Infidel on that dear, old battlefield
And though his steel sliced my flesh, I refused to retreat or yield.

Many cold nights in the darkness I sobbed there in my cave,
Crying out for the Passion and the temptations of the grave,
I walked naked in the snow and with branches lashed my back,
I slept on a cold, hard stone wearing a woolen burlap sack.
With Love I preached to the animals, their eyes brightly glistened,
Yet it was to the people I spoke, though they pretended not to
listen.

In the monastery at Lhasa I mastered the secrets of how to heal,
I chanted slowly through the night, carving images upon the wheel,
I perfected the secrets of Tantra and merged quietly with the Void,
But in the passion of that ecstasy, my own destiny was destroyed
For, along the road I traveled, God Himself lay sick and in pain,
Yet I refused to bend and heal Him and that shall ever be my
shame.

So many comings and goings, so much Destiny and Fate!
So much love and longing; the constant striving to be great,
So many difficult lessons, so much Truth to know,
Every opportunity to learn them, every chance to grow,
Then at that moment of intensity, I ignored the gift of the Divine,
I lost the touch of Humanity and threw my Divinity before the
swine.

I stood upright once again, though I started as a thief,
Then the True Guru, by His Grace, brought my Soul relief,
But it was His beautiful son I served, for all my passing days,
Who raised me in my consciousness and I left my thieving ways,
Except for that risky business that took me to Lahore,
But I brought them safely back to my Beloved Guru's door.

Another click of the hub, another slow turn of the wheel,
Now and then, and from time to time, these are the things I feel
In the fog of distant memory, blurred between my dreams,
The continuous thread of Soul and Thou weaves between the seams
Of this tapestry, which is woven upon the loom of Grace,
The Master Weaver binds us together, tightly with His lace.

And despite the rise and fall, the struggle and the strife,
The only thing that matters now is what I do in *this* life,
Its not that dream of past, which hangs like fog upon the trees,
Nor the fantasy of future, which drifts like smoke upon the breeze,
For the rains of madness are falling, eroding away the mind,
And once again the waters are rising; the flood is close behind.

Now I stand in the steel circle, protected from the rains
And recite the sacred hymns with their hauntingly sweet refrains,
But my chanting through the night will not be counted on the slate,
It's whether or not I deliver that will turn Destiny from my Fate.
Many times we have walked together, many times you've set me right
And this time I'll deliver, with the shining radiance of Guru's Light.

Los Angeles, California
12 February, 1997

MOMENTS OF SIGNIFICANCE

THE RUBY OF THE HEART

*on the occasion of the fortieth wedding
anniversary of Yogi ji and Bibi ji*

For forty years we've stood the test,
We've faced the worst and showed our best,
Given all when there was nothing to give
And showed our commitment in how we've lived,
For deep within this breast of mine
The Ruby of the Heart shall shine!

We stood tall when all around us fell,
We've faced the Heavens and startled Hell,
We lived the joy and felt the pain,
Yet never failed to give again,
For deep within this breast of mine
The Ruby of the Heart shall shine!

We've walked this course, you and I,
We've walked with Grace to be Divine,
We've loved the children; we loved the life,
We've loved the challenge and the strife,
For deep within this breast of mine
The Ruby of the Heart shall shine!

We've fought hard, tooth and nail
And in our mission we didn't fail,
For forty years we've held on tight,
We've kept the Grace and the Light,
For deep with this breast of mine
The Ruby of the Heart shall shine!

Guru loves us, more than Woman to Man,
He protects and guides us by His Hand
And this, our Family, He shall keep
When at last, we lay down to sleep,
For deep within this breast of mine
The Ruby of the Heart does shine!

*Espanola, New Mexico
22 November 1993*

BE WITH ME
Invitation to Summer Solstice

This land is sacred, blessed through the Ages,
It is blessed today by those modern sages,
From the Sacred Well of the Heart.
Here to the Heavens, the Temple of Steel shall rise
Upon this ancient soil blessed by the wise,
For it is here that the Aquarian Age made its start
And it is here that the past shall depart.

At that time when darkness is overcome by Light,
Where the White Hawk soars in his eternal flight
When the songs of Victory are sung,
We come together upon that sacred land
To confirm our Destiny. While united, we stand
With a joyful noise upon the tongue
And together we ascend another rung.

Beneath the deep blue of the sheltering sky,
Which has watched the Ages ascend, then die,
Together we'll make our way.
Beneath the arc of the White Hawk's flight,
Beneath the stars and the full moon's light,
Beneath the sheen of the Milky Way,
We'll gather together in Grace to pray.

The Sacred Science we will explore,
To find the key and unlock the door
That frees the power of the Soul.
We will learn and grow; we will dance and sing,
We will rock and roll until the mountains ring!
We will experience the power of the whole
And rejoice in the attainment of our goal.

Come be with me at the mountaintop,
Your spirits will soar; your fears will drop,
Your smile will reflect the shining sun!
Thousands of souls pray to be set free
And your songs and prayers hold the key
Which unlocks the door through which they run.
My Beloved, the New Age has begun!

Los Angeles, California
13 May, 1996

DICTATION

TO: CMA
FROM: Gurutej Singh, CO, SVP
DATE: 18 September, 1996
SUBJECT: CMA Dictation

I submit myself to the Rule
And in that spirit I took a stand,
Not to appear as a Fool
Or display a heavy hand,
But to give a clear indication.

To act quickly seemed a Must,
For "maybe" had failed in the Past.
So, in order to preserve the Trust
I needed to take action, fast.
So, I drafted the communication.

An important lesson was learned in this way:
To Rule and Deliver, we must Serve to Obey.

PEACE AT GROUND ZERO

On the Occasion of the Tenth
Anniversary of Peace Prayer Day

Here, under the Bomb, at the mountaintop,
We've gathered to pray for the madness to stop.
On this ancient land, sacred for Ages,
Touched by the Shamans, blessed by the Sages,
We pray with our Fathers, we pray with our Hearts,
We pray with our Spirits, for it's here that it starts.

Across this mountain, life as we know it changed,
For there the essence of matter was rearranged.
And all our joy, our hope and Peace
Were vaporized, leaving fear and grief,
And our Sacred Spirit and Invincible Heart
Wept as they tore our dignity apart.

For the Heart is the target, the weapon is Fear,
As the Spirit is bled dry from year to year,
While through Time and Space, we hurl on this Sphere.
Yet we pray, we pray that Peace will appear,
That Grace will return and brush away her tear,
That our songs will rise so that all may hear.

Here we have come! Now let Peace be our song.
Here we have come! Let us sing loud and long.
Here we have come! Let us never forget.
Here we have come! Let us show strength and grit,
For here we have come, united by Prayer,
That soon others will come and join us here.

For ten years now we have walked on this land,
Raising our voices together, hand in hand,
Joined by the vision of one humble man
Who has told us all simply, yes we can,
By the strength of our unity, here and now,
Bring Peace to this planet, if in Prayer we bow.

So, as Siri Singh Sahib Harbhajan Singh
Has brought us together to do this thing,
Then raise our voices now, let the mountains ring!
God hears our prayers, but He *listens* when we sing
Now, let the Eagle rise and smile upon the Bear
And let our unity tighten year, to year, to year.

And when the day is done, and evening's chill has settled in,
Offer one closing prayer, that tomorrow we'll rise, and do it
again!

Espanola, New Mexico
12 June, 1995

THE INVOCATION
for Peace Prayer Day, 1996

Now, let every heartbeat recite the open prayer
With every breath that's drawn from this sacred air,
Let every head be bowed, every hand joined in peace,
As God's sweet, tender mercy causes every pain to cease.
And in this shining moment when we feel His presence near,
Share this precious Peace with those who can't be here.

"Bless this Earth with Peace," is the prayer we all recite,
Bless this Earth with Peace and illumine us with Thy Light,
Bless this Earth with Peace, mending every broken heart,
Bless this Earth with Peace and let the healing start,
For on this special day we pray with every sacred breath,
That life shall be restored, where now there's pain and death.

We offer our prayers with songs, to lift up every soul,
We pray today from our hearts, to be complete and whole
And as we join together to raise our voices in song,
Let this energy move; to bring right, where there is wrong,
Let our prayers be answered so that peace will come at last,
In all our hearts and minds and across this Earth, so vast.

Now let the prayer of every soul longing to be free,
Be heard there in the heavens, as wind rushes through the trees
And let those innocent children who cry in pain at night,
Who live with death and hunger, who hide away with fright,
Find comfort from their suffering and shelter from their fears,
Let Time heal their wounds and brush away their tears.

But let it not end here, let it be carried in every heart,
Let our unity be strengthened in the days we are apart,
Let us keep the spirit alive; let us carry the banner on,
Let every mountain ring with the sweet harmony of our song
And as this great day passes and the sun bows to the night,
Give thanks that we've come together, to spread this radiant
light.

Espanola, New Mexico
14 June 1996

MATA JI's DAY

The Mother of us all is Nature,

        (The power of God through Grace).

The Mother we serve is Liberty,

        (That Sacred right of the Human Race).

The Mother we honor is she who bore us,

        (Who drew milk from her own blood).

So on this day let us bow with reverence,

        (As grateful children should),

And respect our Mother Nature,

        (Pledging ourselves to Mother Liberty's

        light)

That the children of the Mothers beside us

        (Can have a future that shines bright!)

        Los Angeles, California
        2 May, 1996

185

THE SUN SHALL RISE
On the Occasion of the Dedication of the Langar Hall

"The Sun Shall rise in the West," he said.
The proof is here on this sacred ground,
The cornerstone of the future is laid,
For here the sons and daughters are found
Of Him, who gave us that primal sound.

From this earth the spirit shall ascend,
To light the lamp of the Aquarian Age,
And to that invincible heart He shall bend
To write this story upon history's page,
That pain and suffering shall be assuaged.

The living miracle of the Fourth Guru
Is standing before us, for all to see.
It is not we who are great but what we do,
For Guru's miracle has caused this to be
And it is Guru's wisdom that keeps us free.

Many have come and many shall go
And still, many more shall come again,
But those who have come to bow down low,
Who step with reverence and enter in,
Shall leave a legacy that will never end.

Espanola, New Mexico
11 October, 1995

OUR WEDDING

On the occasion of the marriage of
Karam Singh and Sat Bir Kaur

I cannot say that I love you,
Because I don't know what that means,
Today, I can only walk with you,
To share our longings, hopes and dreams.
Now, we step out not understanding
The reality of what we are doing.
Walk with me now, through these four turns.

Today we sit here together
And before our family we take a vow,
To serve each other forever,
Then to the Guru we turn and bow,
It is Love and Grace that brought us here,
Let us pray that sustains us year to year.
Walk with me now, through these four turns.

Only our prayers will inspire us
Through the challenges that lie ahead,
Now we hold the shawl between us,
As we are joined by Guru's thread,
For this shawl represents the tether
That will hold us through Life, together.
Walk with me now, through these four turns.

Human love is fickle and shallow,
We fall in and out of love each day.
Without depth our marriage will be hollow,
We will slip, lose our grip and fall away.
Guru's instructions will guide us through life;
That will nurture us through our times of strife.
Walk with me now, through these four turns.

Commitment is the solution to our problems.
Without commitment, all Love would be lost,
We commit ourselves now to resolve them,
No matter the sacrifice or cost.
Love, which is God, will grow in us,
As His mercy today shines on us.
Walk with me now, through these four turns.

So, we will rise together each morning
And we will lie together every night,
To our Guru we will tie our mooring
And pray that his Hand holds it tight.
All of our life lies before us today,
Together we will build it in Guru's way.
Walk with me now, through these four turns.

Espanola, New Mexico
15 January, 1995

TIME

New Year's Greeting 1996

As the New Year turns before us,
As the Past Year dims, then fades,
As songs of joy rise from the chorus
And the glow of Hope shines in all shades,
Let us together now bow as friends
And pray, from our hearts, for the coming year.
And then, before the old year ends,
Let us give thanks for all that's dear,
To the One who has brought us here
And by Who's Grace we have passed this year.

May you find Peace by the works of your hands,
May the Prayer of your heart bring you Grace,
May God's Peace prevail and hold in all lands,
May His Light shine brightly, on each face,
May the Gift of Success ever be with you,
May you grow in the coming year,
May the Gift of Laughter see you through,
That you overcome all that you fear
And hold your loved ones dear,
In this and every year.

Espanola, New Mexico
18 December, 1995

SIBLINGS OF DESTINY

SIBLINGS OF DESTINY

He stepped out of the river and walked upon the land,
"There is One God," is what he said, "To this Truth I set my hand,
Jap is the way to know Him; there is no other way to understand,
This Truth was in the Beginning, is now and shall always be,
So come walk this path of Dharma and worship Him with me,
Hand in hand we will walk together as Siblings of Destiny."

Thousands of devotees were with him when he went out for a walk,
They laughed and sang and hung around, they loved to hear him talk,
Then coins began to appear and the devotees grabbed them without a
balk.
So, at the end of that afternoon only three had continued to stay
And they faced a rotting corpse lying black, there in the clay,
"Who will eat it?" he asked with a smile, and Lehna replied, "Which
way?"

An old man without a Guru sought desperately to be free
From the cycle of birth and death, from life's suffering and misery,
Then he found the loving Guru, who made him a Sibling of Destiny.
Humble Jetha came to serve him as an orphan of the street
And that Light ignited within him, making his soul complete.
Yet, he walked the streets of Amritsar and washed his devotees' feet.

He sat upon the iron plate as it steadily began to glow,
He never stirred or made a complaint, despite the flames below,
Then he slipped into the river and went quietly with the flow.
Those two shining swords came swirling, flashing before the fight,
One held the Akal Takht and one for the Akal Purakh's might,
Then he erected the Baba Atal in devotion to what is right.

The innocence of the animals, the fragrance of the rose
And reverence for all life and everything that grows,
Was the simple lesson that this Sibling of Destiny chose.
Then the sweetness of a child was the vessel of that Flame,
For Truth is not found in books, but in the chanting of the Name,
And though he was but a child, fear and ignorance he overcame.

In that secret solitude the shining Flame was passed,
And before the gathering forces of madness he remained steadfast,
He recited his sacred prayer, bowed his head, then breathed his last.
He gave his head but not his faith, now the die was cast,
For before the Siblings of Destiny the enemy was amassed,
Then the once and future king rode radiant before the mast!

"Have no fear my children, I'll forge you from my steel,
I'll give you your identity, then prove to me you're real!
We will roll across this planet like the spokes upon a wheel!
We are the Siblings of Destiny and by our unity we will stand,
We shall be known as the Pure Ones in every state and land,
For by the Grace of this Sword we'll bow only to God's command.

He came across the water and walked upon this land,
"There is One God," is what he said. "This you will understand.
For the Aquarian Age is coming, forcing you to expand;
You are the Siblings of Destiny, and this time is your Age."
So, we followed him to the future, that humble, iron-willed sage.
Now we, the *Children of the Cusp*, invite you to turn the page.

Los Angeles, California
11 March, 1997

Glossary of Terms Used in this Book

Adi: First, primal.

Adi Granth: The original version of the Sikh scriptures, as compiled by Guru Arjan, the fifth Guru. Later, the writings of Guru Tegh Bahadur were added by Guru Gobind Singh, the tenth Guru, to form what is now known as the Siri Guru Granth Sahib.

Ajna: The sixth chakra or energy center, located at the center of the forehead.

Akal Purkh: The eternal personality of God.

Akal Takht: Literally means, "The Throne of God" and represents the seat of temporal authority as established by Guru Hargobind.

Akal Security: A security services company, founded by Guru Tej Singh and others, in 1980, which employs many members of Sikh Dharma.

Akasha: Ether. One of the five elements.

Amrit: Nectar; as Divine Nectar.

Amrit Vela: 2-1/2 hours just before sunrise, best suited for meditation.

Apana: The eliminative energy of the universe.

Aquarian Age: The time period we are entering into, often referred to as "The New Age," in which the inner awareness and inner self-knowledge shall guide a person's actions, values and decisions in life.

Ardas: A specific prayer recited at the conclusion of a Sikh Gurdwara ceremony.

Avatar: Incarnation of God.

Baba Atal: The second son of Guru Hargobind, who, at the age of nine years old, left his body at will, giving his life for the life of a young friend. In his honor, Guru Hargobind erected the structure known today as "Baba Atal" which is nine stories, one for each year of Baba Atal's life. Guru directed that no building in Amritsar could be built as tall or taller, and today this still remains, the tallest structure in Amritsar.

Baba Siri Chand: The first son of Guru Nanak, the first Sikh Guru. Baba Siri Chand founded the Udasi sect of yoga. He was the greatest yogi that ever lived.

Bangla Sahib: The place in Delhi where Guru Har Krishan, the eighth Sikh Guru, healed thousands of people of plague, taking that illness on himself. Today Gurdwara Bangla Sahib stands on that place where people are still healed by the water from that sacred well.

Banis: Daily prayers of the Sikhs.

Bedi: A subcaste of the Kshatriyas. Guru Nanak, the founder of the Sikh Religion, was of this caste.

Bhai Mati Das: A Sikh of Guru Tegh Bahadur, the ninth Guru, who was imprisoned with him in Delhi, and who was sawed alive for his faith.

Bhandi Chor: Guru Hargobind became know as Bhandi Chor when Sultan Jehangir imprisoned him. When Guru was released, the Sultan said that he would also free anyone who could hold the hem of Guru's dress.

Bidi Chand: A Sikh of Guru Hargobind who served him faithfully and returned to the Guru two horses, Dilbagh and Gulbagh, who had been stolen for the Mogul emperor.

Chakras: Energy centers located in the body.

Chelas: Disciples.

Chola: Traditional dress of the Sikh warriors.

Cusp: The transition period between two ages or two astrological signs.

Dharma: Path of spiritual duty.

Dilbagh: One of the horses of Guru Hargobind, which Bhai Biddhi Chand took from the emperor.

Dukh Bhanjan Tree: The tree under which Guru Ram Das sat, to supervise the excavation of the holy tank in Amritsar.

Essenes: An ancient, ascetic, Jewish order.

The Five K's:	The five symbols worn by someone who has baptized himself into the order of the Khalsa. See entries under: Kachera, kanga, kara, kesh, kirpan.
Goindwal:	The city established by Guru Amar Das, the third Guru, and a sacred site for the Sikhs.
Gulbagh:	One of the horses of Guru Hargobind, which Bhai Biddhi Chand took from the emperor.
Guna:	The primordial energy which makes up the universe contains three attributes, known as 'gunas,' which form our mental attitudes and they are: satvic (purity, understanding), rajas (movement, extroversion, aggressiveness), and tamas (inertia, dullness).
Gurbani:	Sacred language of the Sikhs, based on Naad, the power inherent in the sound current.
Gurdwara:	Sikh temple or place of worship, literally meaning 'the gate of the Guru."
Gurmukhi:	The spiritual language of the Sikhs, literally meaning, "From the mouth of the Guru."
Guru:	"Gu" means darkness; "Ru" means light -- the giver of technology, the teacher. In the Sikh tradition, there were ten human beings who had the consciousness of "Guru." Also refers to the Siri Guru Granth Sahib.

The 10 Sikh Gurus were as follows:

Guru Nanak

Guru Angad

Guru Amar Das

Guru Ram Das

Guru Arjan

Guru Hargobind

Guru Har Rai

Guru Har Krishan

Guru Tegh Bahadur

Guru Gobind Singh

Guru mantra:	"Wahe Guru" is the Guru Mantra of the Sikhs.

Harimander:	Literally means "The House of God." Harimander, also known as the "Golden Temple' is the most sacred site for the Sikhs, and is located in Amritsar, Punjab, India.
Hukam:	Order, command.
Ida:	The left spinal channel through which the kundalini energy flows.
Japa:	Repetition of the Name of God.
Japji:	Morning prayer recited by Sikhs, given by Guru Nanak.
Ji:	Soul.
Jetha:	The name by which Guru Ram Das was known prior to receiving the Guruship.
Jethadar:	Leader or head of a group.
Kachera:	One of the Five K's adopted by a baptized member of the Khalsa; a special type of underwear.
Kanga:	One of the Five K's; a wooden comb worn in the hair.
Kara:	One of the Five K's; a steel bracelet.
Karma:	Action and reaction. The cosmic law of cause and effect.
Katha:	Spiritual discourse, in which stories of the lives of the Gurus and matters of spiritual consciousness, are recited.
Kesh:	One of the Five K's; Long, uncut hair.
Khalsa:	The order of the "Pure Ones."
Khanda:	Double-edged sword.
Kirpan:	One of the Five K's; Knife worn by the Sikhs.
Kirtan:	Singing of devotional songs in praise of God, sung in the classical mode.
Kriya:	Specific combination of a yogic posture, hand position, breathing and mantra; literally a 'completed action.'
Kumba Mela:	Gathering which occurs in Hardwar, India every twelve years, of Holy men of various disciplines.
Kundal:	Coiled hair of the beloved.

Kundalini Yoga:	A science of Yoga, as taught by Yogi Bhajan, that activates the Kundalini energy, which is the life force energy found in all humans.
Kurta:	A long tunic.
Langar:	Community or free kitchen attached to every Gurdwara.
Lavan:	The Wedding Ceremony.
Manji:	The dais upon which the Siri Guru Granth Sahib rests.
Mata Ji:	Respectful term for Mother.
Mohan:	A hotel located in Amritsar, India.
Mudra:	Yogic hand position.
Nabhi:	The navel center is referred to as the 'nabhi chakra.'
Parkarma:	A circumambulatory walkway around a holy shrine, in this books specifically refers to the parkarma around the Golden Temple in Amritsar, India.
Piara:	Literally means 'beloved.' Refers to the five Sikhs who gave their heads to the Guru, on Baisakhi Day in 1699.
Pingla:	The right channel through which the Kundalini energy flows.
Piscean Age:	The age from which we are passing.
Prana:	The creative energy of the universe.
Rag:	The classical musical mode.
Ragi:	Musician who sings the sacred hymns of the Siri Guru Granth Sahib in rag.
Red Fort:	Palace of the Moguls, built by Shah Jahan, where Guru Tegh Bahadur was imprisoned.
Rehit:	The code of conduct for the Sikhs.
Rishi Dusht Dhaman:	Guru Gobind Singh's incarnation prior to his incarnation as the tenth Sikh Guru.
Ross Street:	A Gurdwara located in Vancouver, British Columbia, Canada.
Saag:	A dish made of mustard greens or spinach.
Sadhana:	Daily spiritual discipline or practice.

Sangat:	Holy congregation.
Sardar:	A term used for all Sikh men.
Saropa:	Robe of honor.
Sarover:	A pool or lake. The most famous sarover is that surrounding the Golden Temple in Amritsar India, a dip in which is said to remove one's afflictions.
Seva:	Selfless service.
Shabd:	The sound; sound current.
Shabd Guru:	The Guru of the Sound Current.
Shuni Mudra:	A hand position used in meditation where the middle finger (Saturn finger) touches the tip of the thumb.
Shunyia:	The state of zero, where mind and body are synchronized at a vibratory level of absolute emotional and mental silence.
Shushmana:	Central channel through which the Kundalini energy flows.
Sikh:	Literally means 'a seeker of Truth.'
Singh:	Literally means 'Lion.' The name taken by men in the Sikh faith.
Sis Ganj:	The place in Delhi where Guru Tegh Bahadur was beheaded. Today a Gurdwara stands on this spot.
Simran:	Meditation on the Sound current.
Siri Guru Granth Sahib:	The living Guru of the Sikhs.
Siri Singh Sahib Bhai Sahib Harbhajan Singh Khalsa Yogiji:	Complete, full title of Yogi Bhajan.
Sodhi:	A subcaste of the Kshatriyas. Seven of the ten Sikh Gurus (from Guru Ram Das to Guru Gobind Singh) were of this caste.
Sultan:	Emperor, ruler, or head of a clan.
Sushumna:	Central spinal channel
Tapa:	Heat generated by spiritual practice, specifically through japa.

Temple of Steel:	Planned temple to be erected at Guru Ram Das Puri, New Mexico.
Wahe Guru:	Mantra or sound current of ecstasy, literally meaning, "Wow, Great and indescribable is God's wisdom!"
Yatra:	Spiritual pilgrimage to a holy place.
Yoga:	The science of union.
Yogi:	A male practitioner of yoga.
Yogini:	A female practitioner of yoga.

APPENDIX:
THE FIVE KRIYAS

Guru Ram Das Kriya

Sushumna

Tershula Kriya

Sodarshan Chakra Kriya

Nabhi Kriya

Guru Ram Das Kriya

MUDRA: Sit in easy pose with a straight spine, chin pulled slightly in. Place your hands in Gyan Mudra, or fold them in the lap, right enclosed in the left, left thumb enclosed in the right.

EYES: Eyes are rolled up or may be focused at the tip of the nose, 10% open.

MANTRA: "Guru Guru Wahe Guru, Guru Ram Das Guru." Recite the mantra in a spoken monotone. As you recite the mantra, focus in the following pattern:

Guru	-	Throat
Guru	-	Heart
Wahe	-	Navel
Guru	-	Lips
Guru	-	Throat
Ram	-	Heart
Das	-	Navel
Guru	-	Lips

Continue in this fashion. At each center, focus the sound there. Keep the chin pulled in towards the chest and vibrate the sound at the throat. At the heart, lift the diaphragm and at the navel, pull the navel in. When you recite at the lips, exaggerate the movement of the lips. It is called the "Kiss of God."

TIME: This meditation can be practiced up to three hours a day.

EFFECTS: The qualities of this meditation are innumerable. It moves the energy around the heart chakra, stimulates the third chakra for vitality, and the fifth chakra for intuition and sincerity. This kriya releases repressed and acquired anger. It brings compassion and tolerance in its place. It can give the practitioner the living experience of the Guru, and the living power of Love.

This mantra is an ashtang mantra (8-beat), and contains the bij mantra (Wahe Guru), which is also known as the "Guru Mantra." It is a japa, not a bhajan (song), so it is recited in a monotone. It can put the practitioner in a deep trance, but bear in mind that the process of meditation is a cleansing process and much of what putrefies below the surface of the mind will come out. When it does, stay focused on the mantra, observe the process of your mind, but don't identify with the contents.

Shushmna Kriya

MUDRA: Sit in easy pose with a straight spine. The hands are in the lap, thumb tips touching, right over left for men, left over right for women. The back teeth are locked and the tongue is pressed against the upper palate.

EYES: The eyes are rolled down, focused at the tip of the nose.

MANTRA: Silently chant the following 26 beat mantra: "Sa-Ta-Na-Ma, Ra-Ma-Da-Sa, Sa-Say-So-Hung, Sa-Ta-Na-Ma, Ra-Ma-Da-Sa-, Sa-Say-So-Hung, Wahe Guru."

BREATH: This is a twenty-six stroke breath, done in the following fashion:

ONE FULL INHALE:

Sa-Ta-Na-Ma -	Inhale in four parts at the throat
Ra-Ma-Da-Sa -	Continue to inhale in four parts at the heart
Sa-Say-So-Hung -	At the navel complete the inhale in four more parts as you focus at the navel.

HOLD:

Sa-Ta-Na-Ma -	Pull the energy up to the crown chakra at the top
Ra-Ma-Da-Sa -	of the head, as you spin the sound counter-clockwise
Sa-Say-So-Hung -	and visualize the energy going out through the top of the head like a corkscrew.

EXHALE: (In 2 parts)

Wahe:	Move the energy from the crown chakra to the 3rd eye.
Guru:	(Without taking a breath), exhale a second time, and move the energy from the crown to the 3rd eye, again.

EFFECTS: This kriya directly stimulates the Kundalini and moves it into the sushumna. With practice, you will become very hot & begin to sweat, no matter how cold it is. That is the Kundalini Energy! This meditation has the power to adjust any disorder of the psyche or personality and can, at a nuclear level, change the projection and mental processes of the individual. It brings a powerful intuitive capacity and saintly attitude, but will put the practitioner through an intensive transformational process. Be prepared for this and stick with the technique.

It is important to eat lightly while practicing this kriya. It should be done on an empty stomach. In the early stages, you may experience a sense of nausea. This is because your endurance levels are low. This kriya helps increase physical, mental & emotional endurance and as you continue with your discipline, the discomfort will diminish. You can practice up to 2-1/2 hours a day.

Tershula Kriya
(SIDH KARM KRIYA)

POSTURE & MUDRA: Sit in easy pose. Bring your elbows next to the ribs, forearms extended in front of you, with the hands in front of the heart, right over left, palms up. The hands are approximately 10 degrees higher than the elbows. There is no bend in the wrists -- the fingertips down to the elbows are a straight line. The thumbs are extended out to the sides of the hands, the fingertips and palms don't exactly line up -- they are slightly offset.

EYES: The eyes are closed, but <u>not</u> rolled up to the 3rd eye point. You are looking at the backs of your eyelids.

MANTRA & BREATH:
Inhale: Pull back on the navel and inhale through the nostrils, and hold. Mentally recite the mantra "Har Har Wahe Guru" as long as you are able to retain the breath. While you are doing this, visualize your hands surrounded by white light.

Exhale: Exhale through the nostrils and as you exhale, visualize lightening shooting out from your fingertips. When you have fully exhaled, pull Mulbhand (pull in on the rectum, sex organs and navel), and hold for as long as you can, again mentally reciting the mantra "Har Har Wahe Guru."

RECOMMENDED TIME: 62 minutes

COMMENTS: It has been suggested that this meditation be done in a cool room or at night when the temperature is cooler, as it directly stimulates the Kundalini and generates a great deal of heat in the body.

EFFECTS: Tershula is the trident of Shiva, the ultimate deliverer. Tershula can heal anything. It's a self-healing process.

This meditation is for the gunas. It brings the three nervous systems together. It gives you the power to **erase your own Akashic Record**. It also gives you the ability to **heal at a distance**, through your touch, or through your projection.

Many psychological disorders or imbalances in the personality can be cured through the practice of this meditation. It is very helpful in getting rid of phobias, especially father phobia. It can be very useful in cases of elimination disorders caused by subconscious blocks. It has been known to be helpful in cases of depression, as well as for person's experiencing sleep disorders.

This meditation is especially cleansing when practiced in combination with a good diet to cleanse the liver. This, along with Sodarshan Chakra Kriya can give one a subconscious overhaul in this time period of the cusp of the Aquarian Age.

Sodarshan Chakra Kriya

Of all the 20 types of yoga, including Kundalini Yoga, this is the highest kriya. This meditation cuts through all darkness. It will give you a new start. It is the simplest kriya, but at the same time the hardest. It cuts through all barriers of the neurotic or psychotic inside-nature. When a person is in a very bad state, techniques imposed from the outside will not work. The pressure has to be stimulated from within.

Tragedy of life is when subconscious releases garbage into the conscious mind. This kriya invokes the Kundalini to give you the necessary vitality and intuition to combat the negative effects of the subconscious mind.

MUDRA: Sit with a straight spine.

a. Block off the right nostril with the right thumb. Inhale slowly and deeply through the left nostril. Hold the breath. Mentally chant "Wahe Guru" 16 times pumping the navel point 3 times with each repetition, once on "Waa", once on "Hey", and once on "Guru" -- (for a total of 48 continuous unbroken pumps).

b. Unblock the right nostril. Place the right index finger (pinkie finger can also be used) to block off the left nostril, and exhale slowly and deeply through the right nostril. Continue.

EYES: At the tip of the nose or closed, as you prefer.

END OF MEDITATION: Inhale, hold 5-10 seconds, exhale. Then stretch & shake every part of your body for about 1 min., so that the energy may spread.

TIME CONSTRAINTS: There is no time, no place, no space and no condition attached to this mantra. Each garbage pit has its own time to clear. If you are going to clean your own garbage, you must estimate and clean it as fast as you can, or as slow as you want. YOU have to decide how much time you have to clean up your garbage pit.

Suggested length for this kriya is 31 minutes or 62 minutes a day.
11 min. a day can build your confidence & capacity to understand who you are.
31 min a day will give you great strength and discipline.
1 year will make you feel fantastic.
1000 days and no one will be able to match your strength!

COMMENTS: If you can do this meditation for 62 minutes to start with, and develop to the point that you can do it 2-1/2 hours a day, (1/10th of the day), it will give you the following: "Nao niddhi, athara siddhi." Nine precious virtues and 18 occult powers. And in those 27 total virtues of the world lies the entire universe. So start with 31 min, then after a while do it for 40 minutes, then for 62 min. Take time to graduate in it.
When practiced 2-1/2 hours every day, it makes out of you a perfect super-man. It purifies, it takes care of the human life, and brings together all 27 facets of life and makes a human perfect, saintly, successful, and qualified.

This meditation also gives one pranic power. It can give one all the inner happiness, and bring one to a state of ecstasy in life.

Sodarshan Chakra Kriya will keep all your chakras open so you will not fall into any ditch. It's better to live a life of courage than to live many, many years like a coward. Courage is in your inner vitality and if your all chakras are open, you will not be handicapped in vitality. You will get the grip on your life. Doesn't matter how bad it is, you shall survive happily.

NOTE: For Pregnant Women: This meditation can be done the full nine months, with no navel action, for 31 minutes daily.

Trikurti Kriya with Nabhi

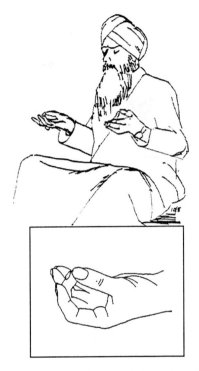

MUDRA: Sit in easy pose with a straight spine. Bend the elbows into the sides, with the forearms extended straight in front of the body, palms up. Keep the forearms parallel to the ground, and parallel with each other, with about a two foot space between the two hands.

HANDS: Bring the hands into 'shuni mudra' -- the tips of the thumbs touch the tips of the Saturn (middle) fingers. Keep the palms face up.

EYES: Roll the eyes down and focus on the center of the chin. Keep them 1/10th open.

MANTRA: Mentally recite, "Har Haray Haree Waa-Hey Guru." Pump the navel in and then release, on each beat of the mantra. Keep the breath long & deep.

TIME: Start with 31 minutes a day. Can be built up to 2-1/2 hours a day.

EFFECTS: This is a most powerful kriya and with practice, it will put you into a deep, calm, trance-like state. The power of the kriya is the power of knowledge and those who perfect it gain the capacity to know the knowledge of another person, plus 10%; to know the contents of a book by holding it, and to gain a deeply intuitive perspective. Yogi Bhajan said he never studied, but instead practiced this kriya. It will give you a deeply stable calm that will sustain you throughout the day. You feel very peaceful, but alert.

This kriya will allow the practitioner to resolve questions of personal identity and elements of personality, which cause insecurity. Pumping the navel point pulls the energy from the lower centers up, to merge with the higher centers where the elevated identity resides. Placing the Saturn energy under control of the Id allows for the elements of identity and the expression of personality to be restructured as a solid foundation for the individual. The result is calm confidence, resolution of insecurities and gender-specific phobias, as well as self-acceptance. Then the superconscious, where all knowledge is found, can be accessed, resulting in the intuitive powers associated with this kriya.

ISBN 155212830-X